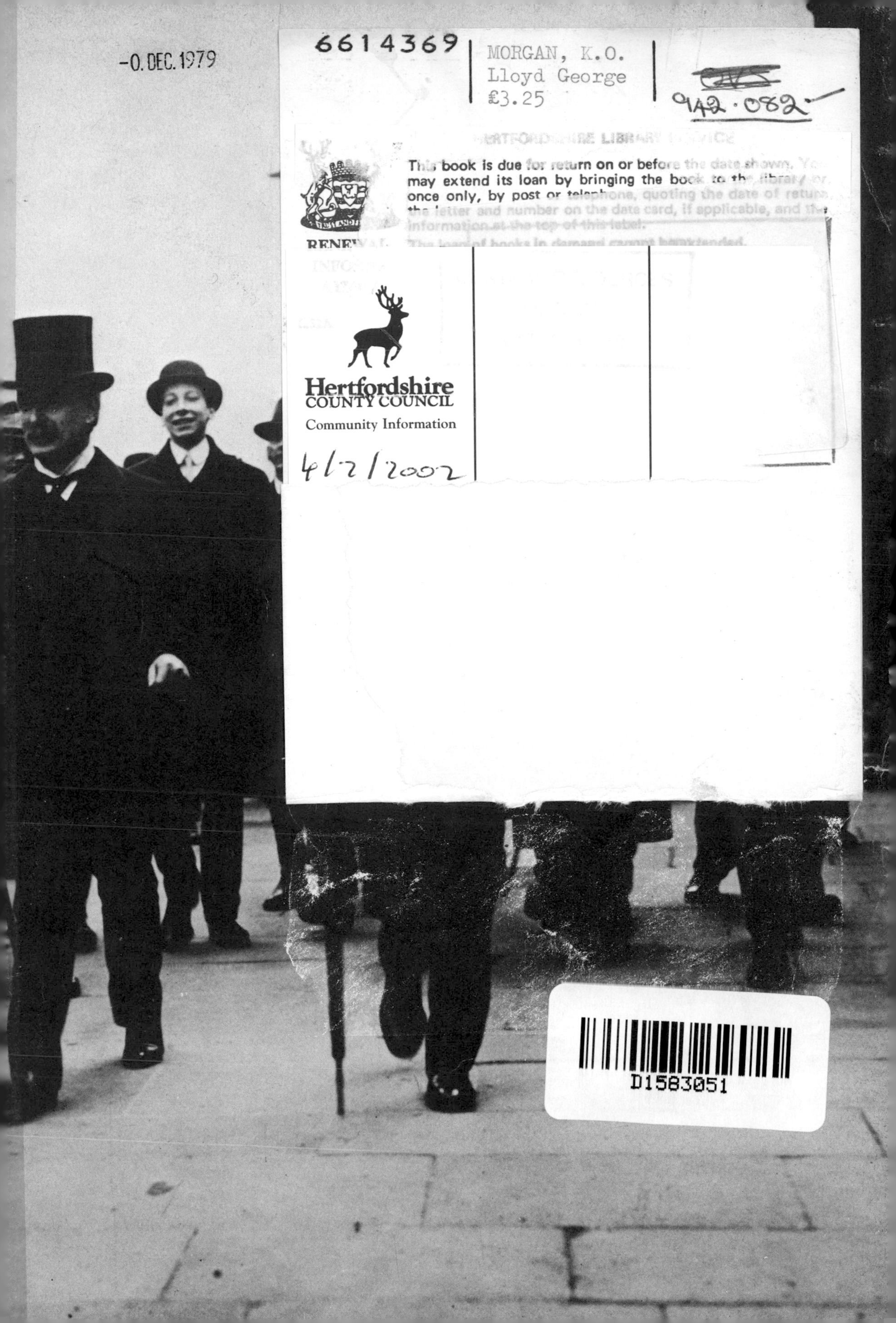

BRITISH PRIME MINISTERS

LLOYD GEORGE

OVERLEAF
Lloyd George in a photograph
by Bassano.

LLOYD GEORGE

KENNETH O. MORGAN

INTRODUCTION BY
A. J. P. TAYLOR

WEIDENFELD AND NICOLSON
LONDON

Designed by Sheila Sherwen for
George Weidenfeld and Nicolson Limited,
11 St John's Hill, London SW11

Filmset and printed offset litho by
Cox & Wyman Limited,
London, Fakenham and Reading

ISBN 0 297 76705 4

CONTENTS

1

INTRODUCTION

COMPARING THE TWO British war leaders of the twentieth century, Lord Beaverbrook is reported to have said: 'Churchill was perhaps the greater man but George was more fun.' There was an irrepressible gaiety about Lloyd George's career even at its most serious moments. Churchill's speeches were carefully prepared down to the humorous touches. Lloyd George's strokes of humour were sparked off by the moment as though some sprite had flashed by. There are few prime ministers whom one would risk recalling from the dead. With Lloyd George there would be no risk. There would be a certainty of vigour and inspiration.

Lloyd George had unfailing zest. This was his outstanding quality. He excited others while remaining calm himself. He had moral, though not always physical, courage and was never dismayed by difficult circumstances. He enjoyed political storms. He knew both how to provoke and how to quell them. But he was not interested only in the joys of combat. He was also set on producing results. Despite his rhetoric and his romantic outlook, he was the most practical of statesmen. He judged men by what they accomplished, not by their rank or reputation. His own achievements were on the highest level. He inaugurated the welfare state. He broke the power of the House of Lords. He led the country to victory in the First World War. He mastered the social and political perils which followed that war. He ended the age-old feud between Ireland and Great Britain. When cast out of office he continued to put forward policies in both economics and foreign affairs wiser and more constructive than those of his feeble successors.

Despite his achievements he was always distrusted by many – a fact that grows increasingly incomprehensible with the passage of time. Lloyd George was a rogue in more senses than one. He did not belong to any of the accepted categories. He differed from all other British prime ministers in his national and class origin – the only true son of the people who has risen to the highest post. He did not respect the conventions of political or individual behaviour. Though always calling himself a Liberal he never put party before country as so many did. In his private life he observed only one commandment: 'Thou shalt not be found out.' He was devious even at his greatest moments. In his own words: 'I was never in favour of frontal attacks either in war or in politics if there were a way round.' Political consistency was not an idea that troubled him, and he was happiest when improvising policies towards an unknown goal. Yet count up all his faults, set against them what he achieved, and it is difficult to resist the feeling that Lloyd George was the greatest ruler of England since Oliver Cromwell.

A.J.P.TAYLOR

I

'THE BIG BEAST' -MAN AND MYTH

DAVID LLOYD GEORGE is the rogue elephant among British prime ministers. Contemporaries called him 'the big beast'. Almost thirty years after his death in March 1945, he retains a unique capacity to enrage or to inspire. No British political leader was more idolised or more venerated during periods of his lifetime. None has caused more fierce controversy amongst historians and commentators since his demise. His private as well as his public life has been fiercely debated. Early in 1973, a television play which cast a jaundiced eye on his character let loose a flood of passionate letters in *The Times*. It is difficult to think of any other prime minister whose character and career could provoke such violent conflict.

In part, this acute controversy that still surrounds Lloyd George's reputation is to be explained by his background. He was a relatively poor man, brought up by his uncle in a shoemaker's home in rural Caernarvonshire. He had no higher education and was never at ease in the 'aristocratic embrace' of court or country. He was to react fiercely against a visit to Balmoral in 1911. 'The whole atmosphere reeks with Toryism. I can breathe it and it depresses and sickens me' (letter to Mrs Lloyd George, 16 September 1911). He was self-consciously Welsh and Welsh-speaking, a Baptist who totally rejected the establishment in church or state, a self-made man in a world run by the English power élite. It was a world he was to conquer. He thrust his way to the summit by his own energy, gifts and ambition. But the Welsh outsider he remained to the end.

Still, the controversy that his career has aroused has deeper roots than this. After all, there were many other self-made nonconformists in politics – some also from Wales. A nonconformist Welshman like Tom Ellis never stirred up the same passions as did Lloyd George, for Lloyd George also possessed unique personal qualities that gave his stormy political odyssey a character all its own. In a special sense, he lay outside the mainstream of British politics. His career was an unusually long one – he sat in the House of Commons for almost fifty-five years (1890 to 1945) – and went through many shifts of attitude. It was marked by apparently inexplicable contradictions. He was the pro-Boer advocate of Empire. He was the fiercely partisan architect of coalitions. He was the anti-war supporter of a 'fight to a finish'. He was the old-style radical champion of state socialism. He was the permissive, unpuritanical spokesman for the nonconformist conscience. It is not strange that many contemporaries and most subsequent historians have found it peculiarly difficult to see his career as a whole.

PREVIOUS PAGE Lloyd George caricatured as 'the Welsh Wizard'.

OPPOSITE Punch cartoon of 1910. Lloyd George's Welsh background was never forgotten, either by him or the press.

THE ARCH-DRUID OF DOWNING STREET.

A Musical Correspondent at the Eisteddfod writes.—"Mr. Lloyd George then obliged with '*Land of My Fathers.*' The Chancellor of the Exchequer, in his rendition of the famous Land song, gave its full site value to every note."

Beyond this, he was a uniquely complex, many-sided man. Some, indeed, concluded that he had no fixed views of any kind. Keynes, in a bitter essay first written after the Paris peace conference in 1919, but suppressed from publication until 1933 (by which time Keynes had been reunited with Lloyd George and then had quarrelled with him again), described him as 'rooted in nothing'. Perhaps the truth was rather that Lloyd George was rooted in a world unknown to a Cambridge don who sought the rarefied company of the 'Bloomsbury set' – rooted in the earthy, democratic culture of rural Wales in the late nineteenth century. The point was put much more kindly by the American ambassador to Britain, Walter Hines Page, in 1917. Page, a

ABOVE LEFT Golf was Lloyd George's favourite game and his main means of escape from the pressures of political life.

ABOVE A crowd follows Lloyd George along Downing Street during the coal strike of 1912. At this period Lloyd George won much popularity for his skilful handling of industrial disputes.

great admirer of the prime minister, wrote: 'Oh, he's truthful, perfectly truthful. But a Scotchman's truth is a straight line. A Welshman's is more of a curve.' As Lloyd George climbed to the pinnacle of power, so the air of mystery surrounding him continued to build up. He was passionately idolised, never more so than at the end of the First World War in 1918. Yet he was no less bitterly distrusted, especially in the last phase after his downfall as prime minister in 1922. To the end, he seemed elusive, defying ultimate explanation. There was about him, Harold Nicolson wrote, 'an aroma of secrecy'. Someone once asked in this later period, 'What is Lloyd George like when he is alonc in the room?' The answer, a cruel one, was that 'When

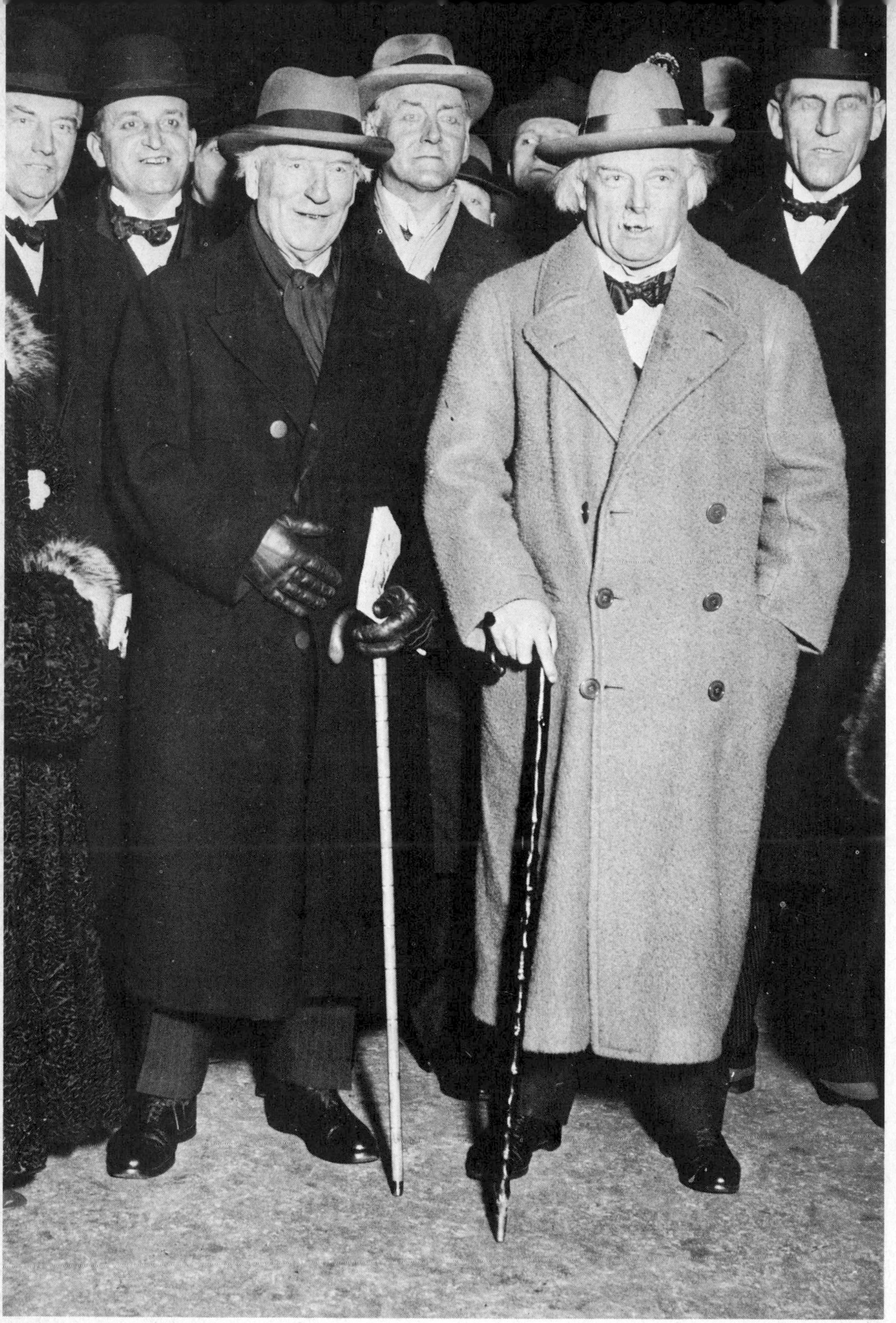

Lloyd George is alone in the room, there's nobody there'. Over the truth of this verdict, political commentators are still fiercely contending.

As a result of this complex background and personality, Lloyd George's historical reputation has gone through kaleidoscopic changes. It is not in the least surprising that there is as yet no thoroughly satisfactory biography covering his whole career in any depth. Until his downfall as prime minister in 1922, most of the studies of him, especially the biographies, were romantic and unreal. They were often written by Welshmen like J. Hugh Edwards and Beriah Gwynfe Evans, products of the same democratic radicalism that had moulded Lloyd George himself. They usually viewed his career, to use the title of Hugh Edwards's biography in 1908, as a tale of Lloyd George's progress 'from village green to Downing Street', on the lines of the sentimental 'log cabin to president' stories current in the United States. In these biographies Lloyd George is depicted as the poor boy from remote Llanystumdwy, emerging as the hammer of the 'unholy trinity' of the bishop, the brewer and the squire, as the champion of Wales and the messiah of the underprivileged. When war broke out in 1914, some of these Liberal admirers were somewhat uncertain about the new directions in which his career now appeared to be moving, especially about his new association with the Tories and his part in the fall of Asquith in December 1916. Even so, right down to the last months of his premiership, there seemed to be clear signs that his radical credentials were being maintained, and that he remained loyal to the faith of his Welsh forefathers.

At the same time, the latter period of his premiership from 1919 onwards saw the rise of a new, bitterly hostile critique of his career which for the next forty years dominated the popular mind just as completely as the earlier romantic versions had done. Lloyd George had always been a tough, belligerent man: the Liberal journalist, A. G. Gardiner, had written of him in 1914 (in *Pillars of Society*): 'The fundamental fact about Mr. George is that he is above all a fighter.' Lloyd George's private correspondence is littered with the verb 'to smash': now this aggressiveness reaped its harvest. The new tone was set by a speech in which Baldwin described him as 'a dynamic force' who had smashed the Liberal Party and might well do the same to the Conservatives; and 'a dynamic force', Baldwin added, 'is a very terrible thing'. During the 1920s, his attack was echoed by partisans of Asquith, convinced that Lloyd George's

OPPOSITE Lloyd George with Asquith, whose downfall in 1916 was for many years blamed by hostile critics on Lloyd George's own machinations.

intrigues had overthrown their hero in 1916 and divided their party ever since. They added their voices to the tirade of criticism, while Lloyd George's Coalition Liberal supporters were largely silent. Keynes's hostile essay, which appeared in 1933, as mentioned above, confirmed this new view of Lloyd George as an unprincipled adventurer who would sacrifice his friends and his beliefs to perpetuate himself in office.

Nor were the other political parties any more sympathetic to Lloyd George in the post-1922 period. Labour men remembered him less as the creative social reformer of the years 1908 to 1914 (and, indeed, of the years 1925 to 1929) but rather as the head of a post-war government which had deceived the miners, accused Labour leaders of being Bolshevik agents, and challenged the unions to the confrontation of a general strike.

Lloyd George in 1918, still at the height of his popularity, receiving a bouquet from old age pensioners of Morriston, Wales.

Whereas he was seen by Labour men as the symbol of right-wing reaction and nationalism, Conservatives in the Baldwin–Chamberlain era viewed him as a rootless radical, one who had flouted orthodox conventions time and again, who had traded honours and peerages, who had wielded supreme prime ministerial power, who had negotiated with press lords and business tycoons rather than with Cabinet colleagues, and who had challenged every tradition of the British constitution. The fact that Lloyd George's government in 1918 to 1922 also brought peace to Ireland, some pacification to Europe and social reform for the masses hardly endeared him to the Conservative conscience either. In short, for the left and for the right, Lloyd George became a convenient whipping-boy for all the ills from which Britain in the inter-war period was ailing.

Lloyd George's famous powers of oratory drew immense crowds, even after his active political life was over. Here he strikes a characteristic pose during a speech to Suffolk farmers in 1930.

OPPOSITE Lloyd George in later life. Always conscious of his appearance, as an old man he is reported to have rinsed his hair with egg-white to enhance its whiteness.

In less than twenty years, he had slipped from superman to scapegoat, with no fixed abode in public life.

After his death in 1945, the torrent of abuse and vilification directed against Lloyd George continued to mount. Several biographies of his career failed to stem the tide. The best of them, Thomas Jones's book in 1951, admirable in many ways, was too cold and impersonal, too much the view of the man from Whitehall. Lord Beaverbrook's captivating accounts of the politics of 1914 to 1922 ended with the verdict that Lloyd George sought power only for its own sake, that he wanted sole occupation of the 'driver's seat', and was careless of the direction in which the vehicle was going. Further, new revelations from those close to Lloyd George threw doubt on his private life. It had long been known that his first marriage to Dame Margaret eventually became unhappy and that he had been associated mainly with his secretary, Frances Stevenson, from 1913 onwards: she became his second wife in 1943. This was expanded in a book in 1960 by the second Earl Lloyd George into a description of Lloyd George as an amorous libertine who pursued women with the relentless passion of a Bluebeard. Donald McCormick in 1963 claimed that Lloyd George was typical of the 'sultry, sexual evangelism of the Welsh valleys', where 'nonconformity and lust stalked hand in hand' (*The Mask of Merlin*). Until the mid-1960s these versions of Lloyd George's career prevailed. His reputation as man as well as statesman was at a low ebb.

Since then, however, there has been a significant change. A flood of new material has become available. We now have the superbly catalogued Lloyd George papers in the Beaverbrook Library in London which contain massive documentation for his career after December 1916. There have been published volumes of primary sources relating to his life with his first wife, Dame Margaret, and with Frances Stevenson. Even more important, historians, especially younger ones, seem prepared to look at Lloyd George's career as a whole, with more objectivity and less inclination to indulge in superfluous moralising. For them, perhaps, to be a historian is not necessarily to play the hanging judge. It may indeed be that a generational change is occurring in tune with a more tolerant or permissive climate of opinion. Perhaps younger writers look with more sympathy on one who was essentially a great rebel and a great critic, who stood outside the established institutions and vested interests and who yet had definable long-term objectives in terms of social reform and international peace.

Lloyd George will never again be portrayed as the unreal 'tribune of the people' of the romantic idylls of pre-1922. He will be portrayed faithfully, warts and all, without illusion or sentiment. But, if history is not served by uncritical eulogy, neither is it helped by mindless abuse. It seems equally unlikely that future historians will return to the denigration that assailed the man in the years between the 1920s and the 1960s. Quite simply, we now know too much about his career and beliefs to dismiss them in so simple a way. He will never be an easy figure to sum up. He will always remain amongst the most complex of politicians and of prime ministers. He can never be easily categorised as 'right' or 'left'. An ultimate understanding may always elude the historian. But it seems safe to say that the study of Lloyd George is now emerging from pre-history into history. A more complete, fairer and more satisfying picture of a remarkable and creative political genius is gradually being pieced together, though it will take much careful and laborious research by scholars present and future to fill out the picture in detail. This book has been written in the modest hope that it may help others to continue this process of objective inquiry.

2

THE GRASS ROOTS
1863-1902

ALTHOUGH LLOYD GEORGE was associated with Wales throughout his public career, he was born in England, at 5 New York Place, Chorlton-upon-Medlock, Manchester, on 17 January 1863. A plaque on a nearby council house now commemorates the event. He made play with his origins as 'a Lancashire lad' whenever he later made speeches in the industrial north-west. His family background was a relatively secure middle-class one, contrary to the accounts of many later admirers. His father, William George, a Pembrokeshire man from yeoman stock, was a schoolmaster and at one time in charge of a Unitarian school in Liverpool. He was a friend of the Unitarian leader, James Martineau. Lloyd George's own religious views in later life often reflected the deist, rationalist beliefs of his father, but they never knew each other, for William George died of pneumonia when David was but eighteen months old. With his widowed mother, Elizabeth Lloyd, a Caernarvonshire woman, and his elder sister, Mary Ellen, the young child was taken to Llanystumdwy, a small village on the river Dwyfor near Criccieth in southern Caernarvonshire. A few months later the family was increased by the birth of Lloyd George's younger brother, William. In Llanystumdwy they were brought up by the celebrated 'Uncle Lloyd' – Richard Lloyd, a self-employed shoemaker, a stern radical and a lay preacher in the Campbellite Baptist church. Much romance has attached to the relationship between Uncle Lloyd and his favourite nephew. Undoubtedly Lloyd George's career gained a momentum of its own after he entered parliament, and his uncle's guidance became of lesser importance. But there is no case for doubting that Uncle Lloyd, and the democratic Welsh values that he represented, were the dominant formative influences of young David's career. 'All that is best in life's struggle I owe to him first,' wrote Lloyd George to his wife in 1902, and there is no reason to question his sincerity. Uncle Lloyd symbolised a decisive and consistent thread in Lloyd George's progress until he attained the premiership. When the old man died, at the age of eighty-three in February 1917, Lloyd George was shattered by grief. Perhaps he sensed that something of his Welsh roots had died with his uncle.

The first twenty-seven years of Lloyd George's life have been chronicled often enough, and the main outlines are a familiar story. They are the very stuff from which romantic legends are made. He entered the local village school at Llanystumdwy where he stayed until he was thirteen. Here he was superbly taught in rudimentary mathematics, geography and scripture

PREVIOUS PAGE Lloyd George's birthplace at 5 New York Place, Manchester.

ABOVE Elizabeth Lloyd and William George, the parents of Lloyd George. RIGHT Lloyd George (left) aged three with his elder sister Mary Ellen.

The cottage of Lloyd George's uncle, Richard Lloyd, in Llanstumdwy, where Lloyd George grew up.

by the headmaster, David Evans. But it was an Anglican school and this fanned the early anti-clericalism of Uncle Lloyd's devoted Baptist nephew. He led a 'strike' of the schoolchildren when they were required to recite the Anglican catechism before the local gentry. When William broke the silence by intoning 'I believe', he received a sound thrashing from his militant elder brother. In 1877 David Lloyd George was articled to a local solicitor's firm in nearby Portmadoc: Breese, Jones and Casson. Finally in 1884 he passed his law examination (with only third-class honours) and was able to set up practice on his own in Criccieth. It was a perfect base for a future political career.

Another major personal landmark followed shortly afterwards, when he began to court Margaret Owen, the only daughter of a prosperous Methodist farmer who lived near Criccieth. The Owen family were very far from being enthusiastic about Lloyd George as a suitor for the hand of their daughter. They were respectable Methodists, Lloyd George a Baptist and an adherent of the radical Campbellite wing at that. The Owens were people of property and read with alarm

of the young Criccieth solicitor's public attacks on the gentry, the Church and the establishment in general. Nor did Uncle Lloyd, on his side, favour Margaret Owen as a possible wife for David, and tried to divert his nephew's gaze to eligible Baptist girls in the Criccieth neighbourhood. So Lloyd George's courtship of Margaret Owen was a long and complicated affair which called for all his proven qualities of diplomacy and guile, already apparent even at this early stage. Sympathetic farm servants smuggled in messages to Miss Owen during the daytime, while midnight assignations were frequent. Eventually they were married in January 1888 and for many years were exceptionally happy. Their first child, Richard, was born to them in February 1889. In view of the exaggerated attacks that were later made on Lloyd George's moral standards, insinuating that he was casual and even lustful in his relations with women, it is perhaps worth laying some stress on Lloyd George's enduring relationship with his first wife. They shared many interests, such as a love of the theatre and of pulpit oratory. Further, Margaret was an important element in his early political progress. Quite apart from providing a secure haven

Portmadoc High Street at the turn of the century, the site of Messrs Breese, Jones and Casson, the solicitors to which Lloyd George was articled in 1877.

of domestic peace, she also represented the earthy, simple culture of the Welsh countryside, which provided the mainspring of her husband's political faith.

However, what is most important about these early years are the steps which led Lloyd George towards a career in politics. From his early childhood he was passionately absorbed in political events: indeed, an important key to his later premiership lies in his unique involvement with political personalities and issues to the exclusion of almost everything else. Further, he felt early on that he had a special destiny or mission in public affairs. He wrote to Margaret Owen before their marriage: 'I am prepared to thrust even love itself under the wheels of my Juggernaut if it obstructs the way.' He added: 'I must not forget that I have a purpose in life. And however painful the sacrifice I may have to make to attain this ambition I must not flinch.'

As a small child, he was deeply stirred by the radical passions that were agitating rural Wales in the 1870s – the new democratic flame kindled by the 'great election' of 1868, the passionate resentment of the tyranny of landlordism that led to the eviction of Liberal farmers from their lands after the poll. He was reared by Uncle Lloyd in the new concern for religious and political equality, for social justice and for Welsh nationhood. Even at the Anglican school in Llanystumdwy he developed a bitter resentment of the class system, dominated by the parson and the squire, that enclosed his world. He dreamed of a career which would free the Welsh people from this social slavery. Nothing excited him more during his adolescent years than his first sight of the House of Commons in November 1881. He noted privately in his diary: 'I will not say but that I eyed the assembly in a spirit similar to that in which William the Conqueror eyed England on his visit to Edward the Confessor, as the region of his future domain. Oh, vanity!'

He soon moved confidently into local politics. He was active in the Portmadoc debating society as an outspoken radical. He began to find outlets in the local Liberal press for his attacks on established leaders and institutions. He began to make a local reputation as a compelling orator. In the great division which rent the Liberals in twain in 1886 over Gladstone's Irish Home Rule Bill, Lloyd George almost joined the faction under Joseph Chamberlain which rejected the measure. However, a favourable accident which caused him to miss a train which would have taken him to Birmingham to the inaugural meeting of Chamberlain's Radical Union in May 1886 meant that he

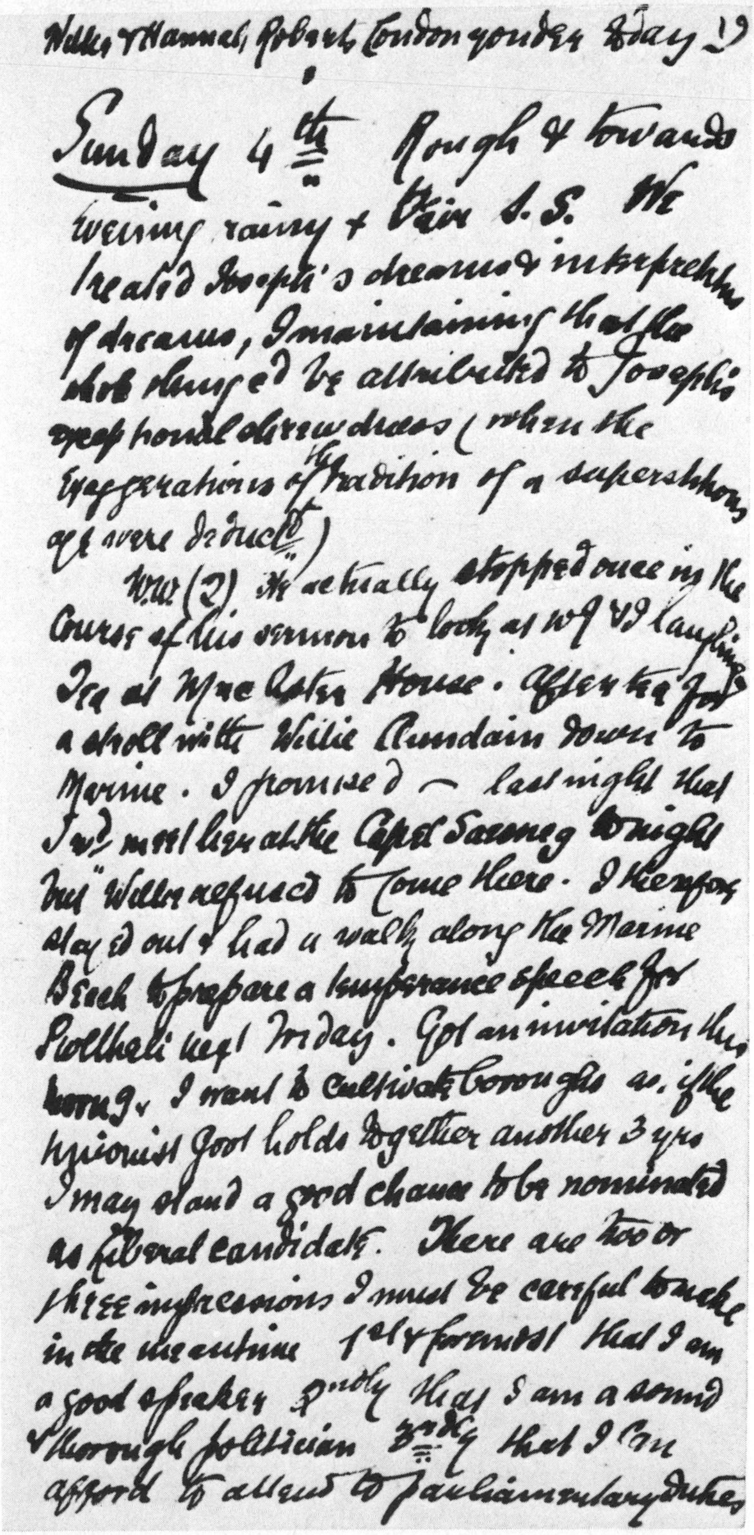
Willie & Hannah, Robert, London yonder today!!

Sunday 4th Rough & towards evening rainy & fair S.S. We treated Joseph's dreams & interpretation of dreams, I maintaining that the whole must be attributed to Joseph's [illegible] (when the exaggerations of the tradition of a superstition age were deducted)

W.W. (?) He actually stopped once in the course of his sermon to look at W & D laughing. Tea at [illegible] House. After tea got a stroll with Willie [illegible] down to Marine. I promised — last night that I would meet him at the Capel [illegible] tonight but Willie refused to come there. I therefore stayed out & had a walk along the Marine Beach to prepare a temperance speech for Pwllheli next Friday. Got an invitation this morning. I want to cultivate boroughs as, if the Unionist Govt holds together another 3 yrs I may stand a good chance to be nominated as Liberal candidate. There are two or three impressions I must be careful to make in the meantime 1st & foremost that I am a good speaker 2ndly that I am a sound & thorough politician 3rdly that I can afford to attend to parliamentary duties

The diary entry for Sunday, 4 September 1887, in which Lloyd George stated the tactics he intended to adopt so that 'I may stand a good chance to be nominated as Liberal candidate'.

Lloyd George aged 27 as he appeared in the Cardiff *Western Mail* when he entered parliament for the first time in 1890.

stayed safely in the Gladstonian fold. It was a fortunate deliverance, since it meant that he remained in a Liberal Party increasingly responsive to its radical wing, not least in Scotland and Wales. It ensured that Lloyd George, unlike Chamberlain, remained for the rest of his career in some sense a man of the left.

After the 1886 general election, in which the Liberals were heavily defeated, Lloyd George rose rapidly to public prominence. In his diary (4 September 1887), he itemised the steps which might lead to his being accepted as a Liberal parliamentary candidate. First, he would establish his reputation as a public speaker. Secondly, he would strive to make his name with influential people by his speeches and articles in the local press. Thirdly, he would attend to his solicitor's practice, and get all his cases well advertised. Finally, he would subscribe 'judiciously' to good causes. It was all shrewdly planned, and in the period 1886 to 1889 he followed these objectives devotedly. He took a vigorous part in the major controversies of the time – the agitation against the payment of tithe to the established church; reform of the land system and fair rents for tenant farmers; disestablishment of the Church in Wales. He was a belligerent delegate to the North Wales Liberal Federation. Meanwhile, in the courts he made his name known as a popular champion of the common man against the pretensions of squires and clergy. Cases of poaching were a particularly useful field in this respect, and he was never afraid to accuse Anglican magistrates of bias. Above all, the Llanfrothen burial case of 1888, in which Lloyd George successfully defended some nonconformists who had dared to bury their dead with their own rites in the parish churchyard, made his name resound throughout Wales.

In addition, he had his ambitious eye on the nomination for the Caernarvon Boroughs constituency, a scattered series of six small towns including his own Criccieth which the Conservatives had captured in 1886. After some local manoeuvring, he was given the nomination at the end of 1888. Two months later, he was elected as 'the boy alderman' to the first Caernarvonshire county council, and was thus involved in that revolution in Welsh local government and society which the new authorities symbolised. The climax came in April 1890 when, in a by-election in Caernarvon Boroughs caused by the death of the sitting Conservative member, he was elected to parliament at the age of twenty-seven. His election was a hard-fought one against a popular local squire, Ellis Nanney, and the margin of victory was only eighteen votes. Caernarvon Boroughs was one of the few marginal seats in Wales, with a powerful Anglican interest in Bangor. Not until the 1906 election, when he was a Cabinet minister, could Lloyd George feel that his constituency was secure. Even so, this by-election in a remote, obscure constituency heralded a career in the Commons that was to endure, unbroken for the next fifty-four years. Lloyd George himself pointed out a possible moral in one of his speeches during the election campaign – 'the day of the cottage-bred man has at last dawned.'

What do these early ventures in politics tell us about Lloyd George's later outlook and conduct as a prime minister? They do, of course, reveal many of the basic assumptions on which his political creed was based. Many of them were drawn directly from his native Wales. For instance, he was from the start much involved with the politics of the nonconformist chapels.

Lloyd George stayed close to Welsh nonconformist traditions throughout his career and retained friendships begun in youth with many nonconformist leaders. Here he is shown with David Davies MP (left), The Rev. John Williams and Ellis Jones Griffith MP.

Throughout his life, he was to retain friendship with prominent nonconformist ministers like Dr John Williams and Elfed Lewis, and to retain his respect for the political influence of the 'nonconformist conscience'.

Again, he was essentially a rural radical, deeply influenced by the conflict of tenant farmers and their landlords. It was a commitment to the politics of status and of social democracy. The politics of class and of economic democracy he seldom understood, since the world of class warfare in an urban, industrial setting was unfamiliar to him. The recent volume of John Grigg's biography correctly refers to some early speeches in which Lloyd George denounced the gulf that separated ostentatious wealth from grinding poverty. But until he became a minister, these were merely general declamations which reflected his hostility towards landowners as a class. Until he went to the Treasury in 1908, he had no clear programme of social reform: disestablishment, church schools and temperance captured his attention in a way that the Eight Hours Bill or 'the right to work' simply did not. It took many years of political education before Lloyd George began to grasp the urgency of such social issues as these. His imperfect understanding of organised labour and of the nature of the Labour Party was to prove one of his great weaknesses as a prime minister, and one of the ultimate causes of his final exclusion from power after 1922.

Tom Ellis, the Welsh radical MP, with whom Lloyd George struck up a friendship in the late 1880s and who later became Liberal Chief Whip.

Another key to his later conduct as prime minister is seen in his early involvement with the press. From his writings in the Caernarvon *Genedl* in the late 1880s, Lloyd George retained an immense faith in the power of the printed word and its ability to mobilise and sway the community at large. He formed, with other young Welsh radicals, such as Tom Ellis MP, a new Welsh National Newspaper Company. Lloyd George himself put up some of the one hundred pound capital towards a new Welsh-language journal named 'The Trumpet of Freedom', which proved, however, to be short-lived. More than any other politician of his generation he was to concern himself with the press, with journalists to some extent, but much more with editors and proprietors. In 1922 it was even to be suggested that Lloyd George might become editor or owner of *The Times*. The roots of all this can be discerned in the Wales of the late 1880s.

The fact that Lloyd George rose to prominence during an immense upsurge of Welsh nationhood meant that, to a considerable extent, he was always to view British institutions and society from the outside. He was never at ease in the patrician embrace of London polite society, and was much more at home among maverick businessmen or journalists, or among his fellow Welshmen. He viewed every layer of government and of authority with a critical, detached eye – the civil service, the military chiefs of staff, the court itself. As the self-made product of a self-made nation, striving anew to assert its individuality after centuries of neglect, he was the very symbol of how a political outsider could capture and command the heights of power. His Welsh origin was an essential key to his career.

On the other hand, these early political ventures show that Lloyd George was also more than just another conventional Welsh radical. After all, most Welshmen proved themselves to be devoted loyalists of the Liberal Party. Lloyd George was very far from being that. It is equally vital for an understanding of his later conduct as premier to see how he diverged from the Welsh society from which he sprang. While he used the chapels as a weapon, in many ways he discounted them. In August 1890 he told his wife how much he deplored 'being cramped up in a suffocating malodorous chapel listening to some superstitions I had heard thousands of times before'. He loathed the hypocrisy of Welsh puritanism, the petty snobbery of the deacons on the *sêt fawr* (big pew). A nonconformist establishment was no better than an Anglican one. He himself had no profound religious faith. Even in the world of the nonconformist conscience, Lloyd George, as befitted a Campbellite Baptist of Unitarian background, was an outsider.

Again, just as in some ways he was a dedicated foe of the landed gentry, so, too, did he respect them as symbols of continuity and tradition in the rural scene. In some ways he thought the squires more enlightened on social matters than were the 'glorified grocers' of the chapels. He could come to terms with landowners like Lord Kenyon to achieve political solutions, just as later on he was to come to terms with Conservatives to forge a wartime coalition.

Just as he could use the press, he was never obsessed with it nor over-impressed by its monolithic quality. It was simply one tool at his disposal. His early letters show a remarkable realism in handling newspapers, using individual journalists to undermine or outflank their editors. He could withstand the hostility of even such an imperious newspaper tycoon as Lord Northcliffe, and could confront without fear the most determined onslaught from the press ever faced by any prime minister.

OPPOSITE Gladstone addressing a crowd on Snowdon in 1892, shortly after the election which made him prime minister for the fourth time.

OPPOSITE Mrs Lloyd George with her five children (left to right) Gwilym, Mair, Richard, Olwen and Megan (in the foreground)

Finally, Lloyd George was in many ways most untypical of the Welsh national movement of his day. He took little part in such typically Welsh movements as the campaign for a national university and a Welsh education system. He cared comparatively little for Welsh literary culture, and, apart from a passion for popular hymns, had little concern for the arts. The national *eisteddfod* was for him a social, not a cultural occasion. He was the eternal freelance in the politics of Liberal Wales as he was to be in the wider national arena. What characterised Lloyd George's view of Welshness as a political leader was its narrowly political quality. Ultimately Wales was a weapon in his attack on the undemocratic political and social structure of the day. He was a Welsh Home Ruler for a time, but had no vision of what kind of Wales would emerge after self-government. Nothing could more surely guarantee the early decline of the Welsh nationalist movement which he came to lead and to symbolise. In the 1880s as in the 1920s Lloyd George was above all the supreme, pragmatic exponent of the short-run. Though he might have added with Keynes, his bitter critic, that in the long run we are all dead.

Lloyd George's years at Westminster until 1896 were largely bound up with the politics of his native Wales. They are of somewhat indirect interest, therefore, to students of his later career. His home life at this period was a happy one. He rented a series of flats in London, moving into Palace Mansions, Kensington, in 1893. Four children were born to the family between 1889 and 1894 – Richard, Mair, Olwen and Gwilym. Lloyd George was an affectionate father when his political duties allowed, with a rare dramatic gift as a teller of stories just before the children's bedtime. He shared in his wife's interest in the day-to-day affairs of the home. At the same time, even in this early period there was a hint of domestic difficulty. It was caused not by Lloyd George's relations with other women, but rather by his wife's aversion to London and her wish to stay at home in Criccieth. By the mid-1890s he had become accustomed to long separations from his family, to breakfasting alone in cold and draughty flats, to spending Christmas and holidays with friends but without his wife. Since his wife was anxious that he should remain an MP which inevitably meant lengthy stays in London, it is hard to place the major responsibility for the later partial break-up of his marriage on Lloyd George. On the contrary, the pressure for reunion with his family invariably came from him. It is not surprising that he felt lonely and deprived as a result, and found solace elsewhere.

He spoke frequently in the House in these early years. He was a bold speaker, not always as effective perhaps as he himself claimed in his private letters. One contemporary, the Liberal member, Atherley-Jones, dismissed Lloyd George's early ventures in debate as 'incoherent declamations'. This is far too harsh, but there is no doubt that he showed a romantic, even careless attitude to the precise mobilisation of facts and figures. His main target in the first two years in the House was inevitably the established Church in Wales. He claimed that the Church Congress at Rhyl had been 'spiced with Romish sauce and Burton ale' and had 'floated on barrels of beer'. His attacks on the Clergy Discipline Bill of 1892 brought upon him the heavy-handed censure of Gladstone himself. Still it all helped to make the young radical's name, and his majority increased to 196 at the general election of July 1892.

After the election, at which Gladstone became prime minister for the fourth time but with a majority of only forty, Lloyd George was in the van of those backbenchers pressing for the government to give priority to disestablishment and other Welsh causes. The Welsh Party at this time included some powerful figures – the radical coal owner, D.A. Thomas from South Wales, prominent among them. Frank Edwards, who represented Radnorshire, and Herbert Lewis from Flintshire were two close allies. The most talented of them all in some ways, the ardent patriot Tom Ellis (Merioneth), accepted a post as junior whip under Gladstone after much anguished debate. In this role, he became a target for Lloyd George's free-lance tactics, and their earlier friendship was severely strained. In April 1894 the new prime minister, Lord Rosebery, made it clear that Welsh disestablishment did not have the main priority in the government's programme. As a result Lloyd George, with Thomas, Edwards and Lewis, led a short-term revolt against his own party whip. Later in the year he struck out into new paths. He broadened the 'revolt' into a wider movement to promote Welsh Home Rule by sponsoring the *Cymru Fydd* (Young Wales) league which would, he hoped, take over the entire Liberal Party organisation in Wales. Lloyd George has often been contrasted with the Irish nationalists. It is said that he sought to work within the British imperial framework while they rejected it. The harsh treatment that he meted out to Ireland during the 'troubles' of 1919 to 1921 is sometimes used to illustrate the difference between Welsh and Irish nationalism. There is something in this, no doubt. But a closer inspection shows that in 1894 to 1896 Lloyd George himself came significantly near to rejecting the idea of working through orthodox party politics at Westminster. So profound was his disillusion with Liberal politics at this time, so intense his conviction that Welsh and other radical objectives were unattainable through the conventional party game, that he was prepared to break completely with his own party leadership and strike out on his own. In May to June 1895 he was engaged in some complex manoeuvres to try to tack on a measure of Welsh Home Rule to the disestablishment bill. It almost resulted in the downfall of his own Liberal government at a time when the ministry's reputation was at a low ebb. To argue that the government might have fallen anyway on some other issue hardly excuses Lloyd George's tactics. Asquith, the Home Secretary in charge of the Welsh Disestablishment Bill, with whom so much of Lloyd George's later career was to be closely associated, frankly accused Lloyd George of disloyalty. 'Peter was a Celt,' Asquith sarcastically observed.

The episode also led to fierce attacks on Lloyd George from Liberal loyalists in Wales and almost cost him his seat at Caernarvon Boroughs in the 1895 general election. Undeterred, he went on building up his Welsh national league as a vehicle of provincial and personal power. It all depended on whether he could win the same enthusiasm from Liberals in industrial South Wales as he could in the north. At a fateful meeting of the South Wales Liberal Federation at Newport in January 1896 he met with the first serious rebuff of his career. He was howled down by Anglo-Welsh businessmen from Cardiff and Newport. They refused to submit to the domination of Welsh-speaking people from the north. They pointed out that the Welsh National League was really only a paper organisation, however much Lloyd George might claim for it. It was a decisive moment. Though he was slow to grasp the point, his career as a Welsh nationalist was substantially over. Welsh values and Welsh sentiment continued to shape his career – Uncle Lloyd and his wife were always there to remind him of them. But henceforth it was through orthodox party politics, in Westminster rather than Wales, that Lloyd George's future was to lie.

Lloyd George's career until January 1896 had been essentially of local interest: he was not nationally known. Not until 1903, for instance, did he appear in a *Punch* cartoon, by which time he had been an MP for thirteen years. In this pursuit of local objectives, notably Home Rule, he had become a feared, even hated man in Welsh life. His conflicts and controversies imposed immense strain on his family back home in Criccieth.

After the 1895 general election, he seems to have suffered a kind of nervous exhaustion which confined him indoors for two weeks and for a while somewhat undermined his confidence as a public speaker. Without doubt he relied heavily on his wife and his brother for support. His wife, despite their long separations, served to soothe the strain and anxiety which had scarred his public life. Brother William supplied something of almost equal importance – a steady flow of income from the family business of 'Lloyd George and George' at Criccieth. In 1897 Lloyd George set up a solicitor's partnership in London with Arthur Rhys Roberts, another Welshman; he also had incidental earnings as a journalist on the *Manchester Guardian* and other newspapers. But he was still a relatively poor man, as he was to remain for many years more, with an income of a few hundred pounds a year. Brother William's careful management of the family firm was therefore a vital support for Lloyd George in establishing himself in politics.

In 1896 to 1897 the family had to endure further pressures. Lloyd George's name was mentioned in a paternity case. Mrs Catherine Edwards, the wife of a Montgomeryshire doctor, with whom Lloyd George had stayed in the past, alleged in a divorce petition that he had fathered her illegitimate child. The case dragged on until November 1897 when it was declared that Lloyd George was entirely innocent; largely through William's skilful handling of matters, he never entered the witness box at any stage. Even so, it was a desperate time for him, and the emerging gulf between him and Mrs Lloyd George became imperceptibly wider. Even if the case against Lloyd George was unproved (and unprovable either way), the affair encouraged doubts about him as a politician of stature. For many years he had been a figure who aroused especially intense controversy. His political approach was intuitive, and erratic. Questions like disestablishment, Home Rule or temperance reform surged to the surface in his mind and were then unaccountably set aside. Political friendships were forged, as with Tom Ellis, and then sacrificed with equal impunity – although Lloyd George never bore grudges and was adept at patching up old quarrels. His financial reputation was also somewhat suspect. His involvement in a doubtful enterprise, the Andes Exploration Company, which attracted public investment in the mythical gold deposits of Patagonia, did not add to his popularity. While many shareholders found their investment to be worthless, the firm of Lloyd George and George was more than adequately rewarded for its legal assistance and advice.

Lloyd George's main drawback as a political figure, however, was that his horizon had been undeniably limited. He was very seldom associated with non-Welsh affairs in the House or outside it. He was little affected by foreign or imperial issues. Defence and strategy were questions on which he had virtually nothing to say. Even social reform, a theme which had caught his attention ever since his youthful reading of Hugo's *Les Misérables* and his exploration of London's East End at the time of the murders by Jack the Ripper, was hardly a consistent subject for his attention. The future author of the 'People's Budget' was in the 1890s more concerned with cutting down government spending, not increasing it. The future architect of the National Insurance Bill still laid emphasis on thrift, private effort and moral reform. Even the industrial valleys of his own South Wales were a world of which he had little knowledge or appreciation. The outlines of a future national and imperial leader were still hard to determine.

But in the years that followed the *Cymru Fydd* crisis in 1896 this picture began to change. He remained a controversial backbencher, and a popular radical orator. But he was gaining discipline and maturity, instead of being just one of those 'harum scarum chaps who occasionally say and do wild things' (letter to Mrs Lloyd George, 2 April 1894). He was more anxious to persuade, less anxious to shock. He began to work with increasing success inside the Liberal Party, newly heartened by by-election successes in 1896 to 1898. He joined the backbench Radical Committee in pressing for domestic reform. The spectacle of his old hero, Joseph Chamberlain, now Colonial Secretary and rapidly losing much of the innovating zeal of his earlier years, warned Lloyd George of the dangers of breaking with the party machine.

In the House, he was now much more effective in linking his concern for Welsh causes with wider British issues. A typical instance came in his sparkling attacks on the Salisbury government's Agricultural Land Rating Bill in 1896. This gave him an ideal opportunity to attack the squirearchy at a time (it was believed) of rising rents and increasing poverty in the Welsh countryside. At the same time, the Bill doled out one-and-a-half million pounds to assist the landlords, including many members of the government, while the condition of the urban masses was neglected. Lloyd George's performance in the House, enhanced by his being temporarily suspended by the Speaker on 22 May, won the warm praise of the Liberal leader, Sir William Harcourt. The *Daily Chronicle* correspondent recorded

William, Lloyd George's brother, who provided him with both financial and moral support in his early political career.

that Lloyd George 'has made the greatest mark of the session on the Liberal side'.

A further effective performance came in attacking an Education Bill in 1897 which aimed to increase grants to Church and other voluntary schools. In the face of Liberal attacks, the government ignominiously withdrew the measure despite their large parliamentary majority. Two years later, Lloyd George's appearance on a select committee to consider old age pensions linked him directly for almost the first time with social welfare. His wider-ranging role in politics can also be traced in his friendships at this time. His early associates in parliament were largely Welshmen, usually faithful lieutenants like Herbert Lewis. Now his circle of acquaintance began to widen. He struck up a relationship with the Irish Nationalist, T. P. O'Connor ('Tay Pay'), editor of the London *Star*, and thus a useful bridge to the newspaper press. He moved in wider radical and labour circles also. He became intimate with Sir Charles Dilke, a social outcast since a divorce scandal a dozen years earlier, but now an important link with the world of labour. Lloyd George became friendly, too, with John Burns, a self-styled 'labour' member and former socialist whose robust independence and vigorous patriotism struck a warm response. Soon they were close neighbours in Wandsworth, South London. Lloyd George's wider outlook in these years, however, should not be exaggerated. He was still heavily involved in Welsh affairs and in essentially rural questions. He had little to say on the great labour clashes of the later 1890s, even the six months' coal stoppage which took place in South Wales in 1898. The only labour dispute in which he was at all involved was the Penrhyn quarry dispute from 1896 onwards, which after all concerned his own county. He helped in the public appeal for funds to support the Penrhyn workmen's committee. He defended quarrymen in the courts when they were accused of rioting. But the strike proves nothing about his attitude to labour and industrial issues generally. It was an essentially local dispute, with an autocratic feudal landowner, Lord Penrhyn, ranged against a small, poor, Welsh-speaking community. Still, however limited Lloyd George's outlook in fundamental respects, it remains true that in the years of opposition from 1896 to 1899 his objectives became broader and firmer, his grasp of political techniques more sophisticated. However erratically, he was beginning to move from the politics of protest towards the politics of power.

There was, however, one significant gap in Lloyd George's

T. P. O'Connor, Irish nationalist MP, and editor of the *Star*.

political understanding so far – namely any consistent concern with overseas affairs. Certainly he was far from being oblivious to the changing pattern of British external policy in the 1890s, especially to the growth of empire. He was never insular in his attitude. His very first newspaper article, in the *North Wales Express* in 1880, had included lyrical praise of George Canning, foreign secretary from 1822 to 1827, for 'prizing the honours of England' and calling in the New World to redress the balance of the Old. He took an interest in the great power rivalries: in the debate over Uganda in 1894 he was amongst those who held that Britain ought to keep her territorial presence in east Africa for political and strategic reasons. During the Venezuela dispute with the United States in 1895 to 1896, he poured scorn on the Unionist government for an apparent craven surrender in the face of bullying by President Grover Cleveland of the United States. He took a grave view of the French challenge at Fashoda on the Upper Nile in 1898. He was no isolationist. On a more personal level, he had travelled abroad several times in the 1890s, notably on a lengthy visit to Argentina in the summer of 1896, supposedly to pursue the affairs of the abortive Andes Exploration Company.

At the same time, his interest in foreign and imperial politics in these years was only intermittent. His declarations in favour of a vigorous overseas policy were hardly a sustained statement of policy. To describe Lloyd George as from the outset 'an imperialist' overstates the case and perhaps underestimates the way in which the simple passage of time could affect the development of Lloyd George's ideas. Contemporaries in general understandably thought of Lloyd George as a politician bound up essentially with domestic and parochial questions, an anti-expansionist, an opponent of increased military expenditure. His friendships were almost exclusively with the 'little England' wing of the Liberal Party, mainly nonconformist; no contemporary account ever included Lloyd George among the Liberal Imperialists. He was suspicious of the deepening British involvement in southern Africa after the Jameson raid fiasco in 1896. In particular, he criticised Chamberlain's policy at the Colonial Office – 'the pretensions of this electro-plated Rome, its peddling imperialism and its tin Caesar' (speech of 4 February 1898). During the Fashoda crisis in the Sudan in 1898, even though a critic of the French, he urged against overt military conflict. Imperial expansion to him was an obstacle to reform at home, not a key to it, as Rosebery and other Liberal Imperialists argued. It was expensive, it built up the psychology

The Penrhyn Quarry Dispute 1896-1903.

Lloyd George's first involvement with organised labour was over the two long-drawn-out strikes of quarrymen working in the Penrhyn state quarries of Caernarvonshire. The autocratic owner, Lord Penrhyn, refused to recognise the Quarrymen's Committee and the workers' cause was championed by Lloyd George in parliament and later in the courts.

ABOVE Lord Penrhyn.

OPPOSITE Quarrymen working on the face of the Penrhyn slate cliff, *c.* 1900.

RIGHT Notice calling for strike breakers to fill the vacant jobs.

NOTICE.

WANTED AT

THE PENRHYN QUARRIES

Blacksmiths, Badrockmen, Boys, Brakesmen, Engine-Drivers, Fitters, Foundry-men, Joiners, Journeymen, Loaders, Labourers, Masons, Machiners, Miners, Quarrymen, Rybelwyr, Sawyers, Stokers, Tippers, &c.

Applicants for work can apply on Monday or Tuesday next (Nov. 30th and Dec. 1st, 1896) between the hours of 10 a.m. and 3 p.m., at the following Offices:

To apply at the Yard Office - -	Blacksmiths, Fitters, Foundrymen, Joiners, &c.
To apply at the Slab Mill Office -	Sawyers, &c.
To apply at Fross-y-fordd Office -	Badrockmen and Journeymen.
To apply at the Pay Office - -	Quarrymen and Journeymen.
To apply at the Pay Office - -	Boys.
To apply at the Marker's Office -	Loaders, Masons, Miners, Machiners, Engine-drivers, Stokers, Brakesmen, Tippers.
To apply to William Parry, Over-looker's Office - - -	Rybelwyr.

As soon as possible after applications to work have been received and duly considered, notices will be posted announcing the names of the men and boys who are accepted for employment.

PORT PENRHYN,
BANGOR,
24th November, 1896.

E. A. YOUNG.

of 'jingoism', it was a surrender to the ruling classes and to Jewish capitalists on the Rand. (Lloyd George was never one to neglect the potential of anti-semitism.) But a more sustained critique of Britain's overseas role he failed to provide, like most Liberals at that period. Such central issues as the emergence of the United States as a world power, the struggles for markets in the Far East or in Latin America, the dangers of 'splendid isolation' in the increasingly disturbed climate in Europe largely escaped his attention. His gaze was riveted not on the 'illimitable veldt' but on the domestic scene, especially Wales.

He was abroad, ironically enough, on a visit to Canada in the autumn of 1899, when the crisis blew up in South Africa and negotiations between Milner, the British High Commissioner, and the Boer leaders broke down. Lloyd George was in Canada, supposedly to investigate the potential of that country for Welsh emigrants, though his correspondence contains little to suggest that this topic attracted much of his time and energy as he travelled across the continent. His visit was rudely interrupted by the outbreak of war in South Africa in October 1899. This is rightly regarded as a great divide in his political evolution. While he retained his involvement with the old radical issues after the war ended – with Church schools, with land and temperance issues, with Welsh nationhood – his political priorities were henceforth never the same. The Welsh radical was being transformed into the world statesman.

Lloyd George's response to the war was decisive and immediate. It was an unjust war, provoked by the maladroit and aggressive British diplomacy of Milner and Chamberlain. It was being fought to sustain the pretensions of a fading squirearchy and the profits of alien capitalists. It would be ruinously expensive and would depress the standard of living of ordinary people in Britain. It would wreak massive suffering upon a poor, rural, God-fearing community in South Africa – a people rather like the Welsh themselves. He reacted with some relish to the early news of British defeats in the Black Week of December 1899, while his children were encouraged to make heroes of the Boer commanders like Botha and de Wet. No less than Vietnam for Americans in the 1960s, the Boer War was a crisis of conscience for Lloyd George. From the start, he had to battle hard against the jingo hysteria whipped up by Chamberlain and the Salisbury government and their largely middle- or upper-class supporters (working-class people seem on the whole to have regarded the war with relative indifference, except in so far as it brought a renewed short-term

Christian de Wet (right) and Louis Botha (above), the Boer army commanders.

prosperity to staple industries such as coal). Most of the Liberal Party in the House reacted equally strongly against Lloyd George's attacks on the war. The Liberal Imperialist wing, headed by Rosebery, Asquith and Grey, gave vehement support to the war on grounds of 'national efficiency'. Most of the rest, at least at Westminster, followed their new leader, Sir Henry Campbell-Bannerman, in giving reluctant or passive support to the government as long as the war went on.

The tide of nationalist resentment in Britain that followed disasters at Colenso and elsewhere, when the Boers inflicted a series of severe defeats on British forces, only made Lloyd George's task all the harder. True, in provincial cities and in the National Liberal Federation, anti-war sentiment was more widespread. The trade unions also declared their support for a peace policy. But in the first year of the war, outright opposition

Cartoon decrying the anti-war stance of the Liberal leader Henry Campbell-Bannerman who belatedly joined the pro-Boers, such as Lloyd George, in 1901.

was dangerous indeed. Lloyd George made his position even more precarious by a series of wounding attacks on Joseph Chamberlain who, he claimed, had made personal profits through the War Office contracts issued to the firm of Kynoch. It all required courage in the extreme. Lloyd George's solicitor's practice in London suffered severely. His eldest boy, Richard, had to leave school because of bullying from his schoolfellows – perhaps his enduring resentment of his father dated from this cruel experience. Even in Wales itself, pro-war sentiment was widespread, especially in the aftermath of the relief of Mafeking. Lloyd George himself had to escape angry mobs in Caernarvon Boroughs, and to endure the insults of 'jingo' critics. After a speech at Bangor in April 1900 he was struck on the head by a heavy stick: only his hat prevented a serious injury and he had to be guarded by the police. Much later (on

18 December 1901) he was to endure an even more frightening experience. A violent mob broke up a meeting he was addressing in Birmingham Town Hall. Lloyd George, disguised as a policeman, narrowly escaped with his life: the helmet he supposedly wore is now to be seen in the little museum at Llanystumdwy.

In this crisis, the support he received from Uncle Lloyd, his brother William and particularly his wife, all ardent 'pro-Boers', was an immense solace. In the 'khaki' general election of October 1900 when the Liberals were defeated heavily, Lloyd George narrowly held on to his seat with an increased majority. Wales, he told the Caernarvon electors in a dramatic address after the poll, continued to march steadily on the road to liberty and progress while England and Scotland 'were drunk with blood'. Had he lost this election contest, it is probable that he would have faced political extinction and would have been forced to settle down as an obscure country attorney.

But in the year and a half that followed the 'khaki election', until peace terms were concluded at Vereeniging in May 1902, there came a dramatic transformation. First of all in the National Liberal Federation, more gradually in the parliamentary Liberal party, the anti-war mood gripped the Liberal conscience. Men like Lloyd George suddenly became acceptable and respected. J.A. Hobson's book, *Imperialism* (1902), was a fierce onslaught on the atmosphere of jingoism. It argued that social reform was essentially the product not of imperialism but anti-imperialism: the Imperialists in the Liberal Party were losing the argument and the initiative. Further, nonconformists and other keepers of the Liberal conscience were becoming sickened by the brutality and violence that marked the later stages of the war. As thousands of women and children died from starvation and disease in Kitchener's concentration camps on the Rand, the war no longer seemed very glorious. Boer 'commando' leaders like Botha and Smuts became popular heroes. Belatedly, the Liberal leader, Campbell-Bannerman, leading from behind, denounced the government's 'methods of barbarism' in South Africa. In effect, he went over to the pro-Boers. By May 1902, when peace finally came the Imperialists in the Liberal Party were a small minority, and Rosebery partially discredited. Few claimed it to be a peace with honour. The anti-war men, after years of persecution, had come into their inheritance. The Liberal Party would never be the same again.

The South African War was a crucial phase in the making of

A Boer family in Johannesburg Camp, one of many concentration camps set up by Kitchener in which thousands died of disease and starvation.

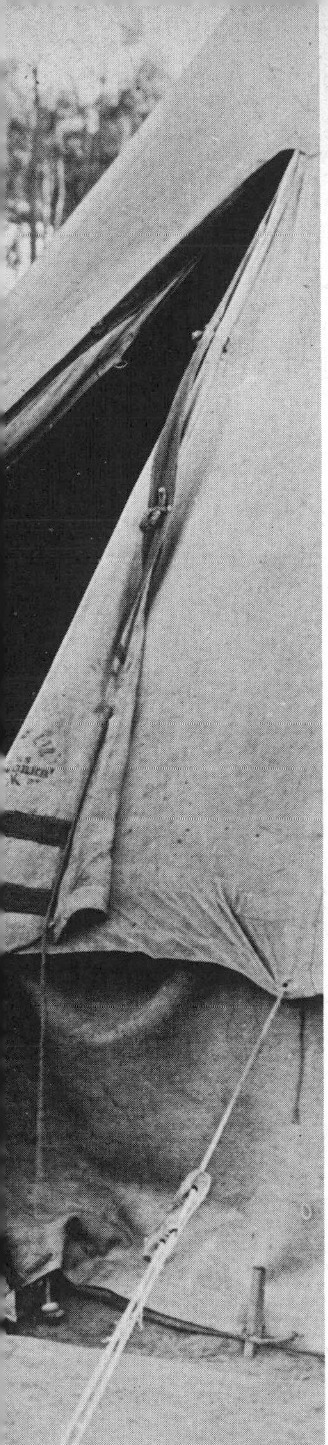

Lloyd George as a political leader. The most obvious feature of this was the wider range of issues that he was drawn into, in imperial and international affairs. His speeches in the house and the country, were full not only of biting criticisms of Chamberlain but also of detailed information gleaned from Harold Spender and other friendly journalists. Lloyd George's links with the radical press were much strengthened, notably with C. P. Scott, editor of the *Manchester Guardian* and (briefly) a Liberal MP, who stayed a firm supporter of Lloyd George for the remainder of his career, apart from a brief interlude during the 'troubles' in Ireland in 1919 to 1921. Lloyd George also reinforced his position as a leader of nonconformity. This was especially evident when he persuaded the Quaker cocoa millionaire, George Cadbury, to purchase the *Daily News*, previously strongly imperialist, and to turn it into an anti-war journal under the editorship of A. G. Gardiner. Although Lloyd George was not a party to the final negotiations, he became a director of the journal henceforth. On a wider front, his anti-war stand strengthened his links with the trade unions

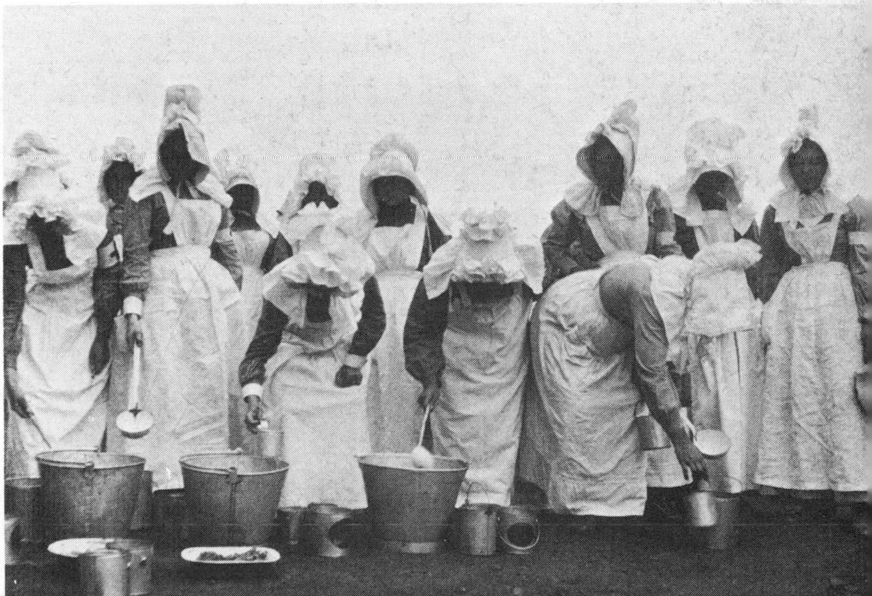

Volunteer British nurses distributing milk at Potchefstroon camp in 1901.

and with Labour. There can be discerned at this time the origin of that close relationship with organised labour which was to play so crucial a part in his later career. A striking indication of his new role was the fact that even the socialist, Keir Hardie, in his newspaper, *Labour Leader*, appealed to Lloyd George to lead a new radical-labour front. This new alliance, Hardie hoped, would graft the demands of the industrial masses on to the old radical base; it would create a new radicalism in place of the old. Lloyd George made no response, but it is significant that he was being visualised, even in this unlikely quarter, as a democratic champion on a far wider platform than that of the Welsh nationalism of six years earlier.

On the other hand, his opposition to the war took on such a form that he was able to build bridges towards his imperialist opponents. Whatever his attitude to the war, he could never be linked with pacifism or with isolationism. He argued that the moral of the war was the need to broaden Britain's position overseas, not to narrow it, and to make the empire a more meaningful entity, based on colonial independence. While he retained his old popularity in Wales and in nonconformist and radical circles, he was finding unexpectedly wide support across the entire spectrum of the Liberal Party. Despite his attacks on the war, for the first time he began to establish friendly relations with leading Liberal Imperialists. He warmly applauded Lord Rosebery's speech at Chesterfield in December 1901 for its statesmanlike approach towards pacification in South Africa and a generous post-war settlement for the Boer farmers. He praised also, in private, Rosebery's emphasis on 'the clean slate', with new social and economic objectives to replace the grand old causes of free trade, Church schools, temperance and local home rule. Social imperialism held its appeal for Lloyd George too. He struck up the beginnings of an unlikely relationship with Edward Grey, an aloof bird-watching Northumbrian landowner, who in some respects shared Lloyd George's own radicalism on many domestic issues. Lloyd George's *War Memoirs*, written in the 1930s, hardly did justice to this aspect of his association with Grey. The breach with Asquith, another Liberal Imperialist, dating from the crisis at the end of the Rosebery government in June 1895, was also on the way to being healed. Lloyd George and Asquith were both struck by the way in which the Boer War showed up basic inadequacies in the British social fabric, by the poverty and deficient housing now revealed and by the poor physical quality of British army recruits. They agreed in seeing and

OPPOSITE Lloyd George holding his youngest child Megan in 1904.

seeking a more adventurous taxation policy as the major weapon for a Liberal attack on poverty and urban decay. Both were to prove outstanding reforming Chancellors after 1905, and to form a brilliantly creative peacetime partnership.

Lloyd George, then, so long dismissed as a Welsh extremist and rabble-rouser, was establishing himself within the broad centre of British Liberalism. He stood at a turning-point in its fortunes. He was a symbol of the way in which the older Liberalism of Gladstone's days could be harmonised with the newer Liberalism of radical reform. Lloyd George had been a brilliant, outspoken critic of the war; but his criticisms had been informed and constructive. He had been an anti-imperialist without being a little Englander. He had tried to link his assaults on a discredited government with a wider analysis of social needs. In a way that few historians seem to have perceived, he represented in a real sense a broad consensus within the Liberal Party, and to an increasing degree commanded its trust. He faced the ending of the war in a happy and secure frame of mind. His family life had never been more contented. The birth of his fifth child, another daughter, Megan – later to be his political heir – in April 1902, reinforced the ties of affection and loyalty binding him to his wife. In Wales he occupied a position of unrivalled authority. Beyond it, he was the confidant for a wide range of Liberal leaders from John Morley to Lord Rosebery. His attacks on the war had lent him a new stature as a dominating parliamentarian. Still under forty years of age, he was seen by the Liberal leader, Campbell-Bannerman (whose own stature was much enhanced during the wartime years) as clearly destined for high office in the next Liberal government. The years of apprenticeship were over.

3

FROM POPULISM TO POWER

1902-16

By kind permission of the Proprietors of "Punch"

BRINGING DOWN THE HOUSE

THE END OF the South African War heralded a happy and creative phase of Lloyd George's career. His domestic life seemed serene and secure. The family now lived at 179 Trinity Road, Wandsworth, and for the first time they had a real home in London. Later they moved to 3 Routh Road, a few hundred yards away. He was probably closer to his wife and children in this period than at any other time. It coincided with a phase in which the revival of British radicalism, after the divisions and strains of wartime, brought with it new opportunities for Lloyd George himself. For the first time he was unmistakably a figure of national repute, as eagerly sought after by the Oxford Union debating society as by chapel gatherings in Wales.

The first eruption of the new radicalism was inspired, strangely enough, by a reaction against one of the great reforming measures of the century – Balfour's Education Bill of 1902. This brought all elementary and most secondary schools under the control of popularly elected county councils. It created for the first time that network of publicly supported schools for which educational reformers had long been pressing. Lloyd George himself was at first enthusiastic. The Bill would give power to the county councils which in most parts of Wales were overwhelmingly controlled by the Liberals. On the other hand the Act stirred up the age-old antagonism between churchmen and nonconformists over the control and finance of church schools. Public funds would be devoted to the aid of Anglican and Catholic schools. It would be 'Rome on the rates', and nonconformists in most parts of England rose up in protest, threatening a massive boycott of rate payment. In Wales the protest assumed a different form as here the nonconformist position was unusually dominant – at least three-quarters of the worshipping population was associated with the chapels. The Anglican Church, 'the Church of England in Wales' as it was derisively called, was attacked not only on religious and social grounds but on nationalist grounds as well. Lloyd George soon found himself at the head of a 'Welsh revolt', the spearhead of a nonconformist revival which regenerated the Liberal Party in the constituencies and at Westminster. The accidental eruption of a new religious revival in Wales at the end of 1904 – much to Lloyd George's delight – added to the new mood of excitement and protest.

But, characteristically, he turned the Welsh 'revolt' into something much more constructive. Instead of the negative, almost nihilist policy of 'passive resistance' (i.e. non-payment of rates) which was adopted by most English nonconformists,

PREVIOUS PAGE *Punch* cartoon of Lloyd George at the height of the acclaim from all quarters following the passing of his Insurance Bill in 1911.

OPPOSITE Lloyd George with his wife and their eldest and youngest daughters, Mair and Megan.

"Onward Christian Soldiers."

Balfour's 1902 Education Bill sparked off a revolt of Welsh MPs led by Lloyd George to protect nonconformist schooling. Caricatured here for exploiting schoolchildren to fight his battle, Lloyd George in fact emerged from the controversy as a constructive radical, and with a much more powerful position within the Liberal party.

he launched a new policy in January 1903 by which the Welsh county councils offered to support church schools, but on condition that certain precise conditions, including the repair of school buildings, were met. This kind of demand was far harder for the government and the civil service to meet. At the same time it raised the education 'revolt' to a higher level of argument. It also made Lloyd George's policy towards education far more acceptable to Liberal Imperialists like Rosebery and Grey. To them, a reformed educational system was a key to 'national efficiency': Lloyd George's policy seemed to combine efficiency with social justice and religious equality. Here again he was strengthening his hold on the broad centre of British Liberalism.

The education 'revolt' also led him in another direction. He began private negotiations with his Anglican opponents in

Wales and with Sir Robert Morant, the civil service head of the Education Department, about a 'concordat' which would set up a Welsh educational council. He established a warm friendship with his long-standing political enemy, Bishop A.G. Edwards of St Asaph, long denounced by Liberal partisans as 'the biggest liar in Wales'. Lloyd George, looking ahead, hoped to bypass the old, sterile arguments about church schools and the 'right of entry' for ministers of religion, and to create a new framework of self government for Wales. As things turned out, the separatism of the Welsh county councils made a common policy hard to attain, while the enduring bitterness over the religious issue frustrated any agreement on an educational council. Still, this attempt to vault over time-worn controversies and to re-cast the discussion in terms of progressive reform and Welsh Home Rule was a persistent theme in Lloyd George's career. It underlined his qualities of constructive statesmanship. It showed that he was a radical with a difference – one who sought power and practical results.

Lloyd George was also much involved in another source of Liberal revival – the attack on Joseph Chamberlain's tariff reform policy launched at Birmingham in May 1903. This led to major defections from Balfour's Unionist government, including in September the resignation of Chamberlain himself. At the same time, the threat to free trade, through the demand for tariffs and imperial preference to meet the flood of foreign imports, challenged a fundamental tenet of the Liberal faith. Lloyd George was foremost among those who proclaimed their undying allegiance to the historical free trade creed of Cobden and Bright. In particular, he liked to take the patriotic line and to claim that Britain had known its supreme days of prosperity and greatness under free trade, despite all Chamberlain's jeremiads. But, yet again, his defence of free trade was distinctive and forward-looking. He was never one to adhere to economic dogma: he was a free-thinker in finance as well as in religion. Free trade was to Lloyd George a means, not an end. It was simply the best available method of ensuring the freest flow of exports from an essentially exporting nation. In addition, and this was a factor which Lloyd George was later greatly to emphasise, it enabled the services provided by 'invisible exports' – freight, insurance, dividends on overseas investments – to be given the fullest opportunity. Lloyd George was beginning to sense the priorities of the 'flapping penguins' of the City and the central banks. Not surprisingly, he maintained remarkably friendly relations with them while in high office.

But to Lloyd George free trade, like every other aspect of the older Liberalism, was expendable. At the Board of Trade after 1905 he was to show every inclination to use the weapons of the protectionist enemy – patents, subsidies to shipping – to sustain British national interests. Later, as prime minister, he was lured by the call of imperial unity, using preferential tariffs as means of achieving this. He was to be very friendly later on with Philip Kerr and other erstwhile disciples of the imperialist proconsul, Milner. Above all, Lloyd George was anxious to show that a mere re-hash of the old dogmas of a hundred years before, casting back to the Hungry Forties and the Corn Laws, was no answer to Chamberlain and tariff reform. There was a need to undertake reform and domestic reconstruction as Chamberlain had advocated. It was the task of Liberals to show that this programme could be financed more justly and more efficiently by direct taxation of the wealthy, including land taxes on the 'unearned increment', than by taxes on the people's food. It was this constructive attitude that was to make him at the Board of Trade and then the Treasury not just a fine administrator but also an outstanding reformer.

Elsewhere, Lloyd George's attacks on the disintegrating Balfour government in 1904 to 1905 followed the usual Liberal lines. He was loud in his criticisms of the 1904 Licensing Act for bailing out the brewers. He was caustic in his analysis of the cost of the late war in South Africa, especially when it resulted in 'Chinese slavery' on the Rand. Lloyd George even outlined, before the startled quarrymen of Blaenau Ffestiniog, the prospect of indentured Chinese slaves being imported into the quarries of north Wales. By contrast, he had still little to say directly on labour and urban questions. He took no part in the nation-wide agitation on unemployment in the 1904 to 1905 period, and was still relatively ignorant of the politics of welfare. Keir Hardie's *Labour Leader* in 1905 attacked Lloyd George, not unjustly, as 'a man with no settled opinion on labour questions'. He still surveyed the New Liberalism from the vantage-point of the Old.

In the autumn of 1905, Lloyd George was recuperating at Rapallo in Italy after a minor operation. His letters at this time were in large measure concerned with such themes as the significance of the religious revival in Wales and the success of the Welsh educational 'revolt'. Suddenly, on 4 December, Balfour announced his resignation. After some party in-fighting, Campbell-Bannerman became the new Liberal premier. It had been widely assumed that Lloyd George would be given

OPPOSITE Arthur James Balfour, Unionist prime minister.

Cabinet office. After all, he was the outstanding young radical in the Liberal camp, a counter to Imperialists like Asquith, Grey and Haldane, and older Whig peers like Lord Ripon and Lord Spencer. But it caused much surprise that he went to the Board of Trade. Probably Campbell-Bannerman wanted a young, aggressive spokesman to defend free trade in that sensitive department. What neither he nor anyone else could have foreseen was the way in which Lloyd George would use his new executive powers to promote sweeping reforms, in a manner unknown since Chamberlain had occupied the office under Gladstone in 1880. When the Liberals were confirmed in office at the general election of January 1906 with a huge landslide majority of over two hundred – Lloyd George's own majority at Caernarvon Boroughs soaring to over twelve hundred – the way was clear for his career to assume a more creative character. For the first time he was wielding power.

Historians have had little to say on Lloyd George's period at the Board of Trade between December 1905 and April 1908. This is surprising because so many major aspects of his political style and objectives emerged for the first time in these years. He proved himself to be a firm and resilient administrator, with a remarkable record of legislative achievement. The Patents Act, the Merchant Shipping Act, the Port of London Authority Act, the Companies Act, the Census of Production Act all rolled massively out of his department. Some of these reforms may have been already in the pipeline. But it required the tactical expertise and sheer drive of the minister to force them through. He showed a rare capacity to charm the House. He had the rarer gift of handling deputations of industrialists and businessmen – 'I found them *children*,' he told Charles Masterman. He could play on their vanity and their fears, and could isolate the central issues in negotiation. He showed an equal capacity for refusing to be overborne by civil servants, even by men as progressive as H. Llewellyn-Smith. He thought they knew little about handling men. And, in the framing of all these measures, Lloyd George showed all his familiar casualness towards Liberal dogma. Indeed, the Patents Act, to protect domestic inventors and manufacturers, and the Merchant Shipping Act, to restrict the undercutting of wage rates by foreign shipping companies, showed a remarkably free-and-easy attitude to free trade. What mattered more than this was that Campbell-Bannerman's government, frustrated and impotent in other aspects of its programme in the face of obstruction by the Lords, had at least one record of outstanding legislative achievement.

Henry Campbell-Bannerman who became Liberal prime minister in 1905 and who appointed Lloyd George to his first Cabinet post at the Board of Trade.

Lloyd George was equally skilful in the other major aspect of his departmental work – the handling of labour. The tact and sensitivity he had long displayed in Welsh politics – for instance, over the 'concordat' negotiations on church schools – was now turned with equal effect to negotiations with the trade unions. Major strikes in the coal and cotton industries came and went. Perhaps the dispute which most riveted public attention was Lloyd George's single-handed averting of a national railway strike in October 1907. He managed to persuade the owners to accept collective bargaining on the railways on a nation-wide basis, with a conciliation board to supervise wage agreements. He also managed to weaken the solidarity of the railway owners by a skilful use of the issue of railway amalgamation. He may have been given too much credit by admirers at the

LLOYD THE LUBRICATOR.

There's a sweet little cherub that floats up aloft to watch o'er the life of John Bull.

[With *Mr. Punch's* compliments to Mr. Lloyd George on his successful intervention in the late Railway Dispute.]

[November 13, 1907.]

time. Certainly, railway disputes continued to plague successive governments down to and after the First World War. Even so, Lloyd George achieved an extraordinary triumph of industrial diplomacy. Campbell-Bannerman told King Edward VII that the country was greatly indebted to 'the knowledge, skill, astuteness and tact of the President of the Board of Trade'. Newly popular with the classes, Lloyd George now strengthened his hold on the masses as well. The railway stoppage gave him a new standing amongst Labour leaders – a vital support in his ascent to the premiership. Not until the later years of his period as prime minister was this 'special relationship' with Labour eroded.

OPPOSITE Due acclaim from *Punch* for Lloyd George's skilful averting of a national railway strike in 1907.

It was a time of public triumph – but of private tragedy. On 30 November 1907 his favourite and eldest daughter, Mair, died of appendicitis at the age of seventeen. A sweet, talented young girl, Mair had always a special place in Lloyd George's affections. He was broken with grief, suddenly bereft and desolate. To Mrs Lloyd George he wrote a brave letter (4 December 1907):

> It was the decree of fate which millions besides ourselves are now enduring. . . . I have a profound conviction that, cruel as the blow may appear & purposeless as it may now seem, it will prove to be the greatest blessing that has befallen us and through us multitudes whom God has sent me to give a helping hand out of misery and worry a myriad worse than ours. I can see through the darkness a ray of hope.

Perhaps this courageous response takes us close to Lloyd George's spiritual beliefs. His dauntless championing of social reform was the political outcome, and the founding of the welfare state. For his private life, the result was less happy. Mrs Lloyd George reacted to the tragedy with remarkable calmness; she and her husband drifted apart far more perceptibly. Perhaps they blamed each other in some sense for the tragedy. When Lloyd George left for the south of France after Mair's funeral, with his two sons Richard and Gwilym, but without his wife, it symbolised the new gulf that was to emerge in his own household, with fateful results.

When Asquith followed Campbell-Bannerman as prime minister in April 1908, it was inevitable that Lloyd George should follow him at the Treasury. Over a wide range of domestic policies, he had established himself as a dominant member of the administration; he had also shone at the Colonial premiers' conference in 1907. He had at once the good fortune of handling the Old Age Pensions measure associated with the 1908 budget. He, rather than Asquith, therefore,

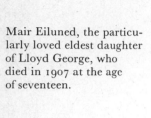

Mair Eiluned, the particularly loved eldest daughter of Lloyd George, who died in 1907 at the age of seventeen.

gained the credit for this long-delayed reform which granted old people five shillings a week. Pensioners would talk of claiming 'their Lloyd George' in years to come. But neither this nor any other issue prejudiced the relationship between Asquith and Lloyd George in the years up to 1914. Asquith's judicious leadership, backed up by stern partisanship, Lloyd George's radical passion, supported by tactical flair, provided a massively effective partnership. It brought Liberal England, not to its 'death' as once was mistakenly claimed, but to its glorious high noon. Those who try to seek a rift between Asquith and Lloyd George before the new strains of the war years will do so in vain.

That Lloyd George would be a vigorous and dynamic Chancellor of the Exchequer was only to be expected. His handling of statistics was often romantic and cavalier but he defended his departmental briefs well in the House, while his political intuition more than made up for his ignorance of public finance. What was much more notable was that he turned the Treasury into a forcing-house for long-term reform as no Chancellor of the Exchequer had ever previously done.

Exactly how this arose is not wholly clear. To claim that Lloyd George was a clear-eyed social reformer from his first entry into politics cannot be seriously sustained, since, as has been shown, his concern in the 1880s and 1890s was with more traditional issues. Social reform had not loomed large among his priorities before April 1908, for all his hatred of injustice and his instinctive feeling for the casualties of society. Perhaps his new advance towards social reform was stimulated by the new joys of high office. Perhaps it was the urge to redeem Liberal by-election failures and to prevent British Liberalism following continental Liberalism along the road of decline and decay. Perhaps, as in the letter cited above, it was the shattering effect of Mair's death which released in his soul the urge to raise up the condition of the downtrodden and the underprivileged.

There was also the important influence of his close friend, Winston Churchill, an ex-Conservative who had followed him at the Board of Trade. In a powerful article in the journal *The Nation* in March 1908, Churchill had pointed the way forward to 'the untrodden field of politics', the field of social reform. By implication, his article criticised the Liberals since 1906 for neglecting their responsibilities in this vital area. Churchill, the manqué aristocrat, Lloyd George, the Welsh outsider, were an odd pair: the 'cottage-bred boy' seemed far removed from the scion of Blenheim Palace. But Churchill and Lloyd George shared a common irreverence towards Liberal orthodoxy. They were equally impatient with dogma and inertia, and anxious to get things done. Together they formed a powerful radical axis on the government's left flank: their friendship largely endured for forty years. It is worth stressing, perhaps, that their relationship was very much two-way. Recent accounts perhaps go too far in emphasising Churchill's role.

Lloyd George himself was greatly stirred by a visit to Germany in the late summer of 1908, and much impressed by the social insurance and labour exchanges that Bismarck had set up there. He also deepened his concern with foreign affairs during this visit, and was anxious to establish a more friendly relationship with Germany after years of naval rivalry. The need for cordial Anglo-German relations is a constant theme in Lloyd George's career for the next thirty years, culminating in his famous visit to Hitler in 1936. He returned from Germany fired with radical enthusiasm, immersed in practical detail about reform policies. He instructed Churchill at Criccieth in what the latter called 'two days very memorable to me'. They worked out a grand design for a comprehensive system for national health and unemployment insurance, and for labour exchanges. These would regenerate the nation. They would, incidentally, also regenerate the Liberal Party, and provide a far firmer foundation from which to hit back at the House of Lords. In the fateful winter of 1908 to 1909 Lloyd George and Churchill worked out far-reaching, long-term programmes

Lloyd George characterised as a highway robber after putting through the Old Age Pensions measure – by which old people were granted five shillings a week.

THE PHILANTHROPIC HIGHWAYMAN.

MR. LLOYD GEORGE.—"*I'll* make 'em pity the aged poor!"

OPPOSITE Lloyd George with Winston Churchill, who had followed Lloyd George at the Board of Trade.

which were to revolutionise British social policy and to transform the political scene as well.

The immediate outcome was the 'People's Budget' which Lloyd George introduced in April 1909. It was, he declared, 'a war budget' which would 'wage implacable warfare against poverty and squalidness'. It created a political sensation. There was new direct taxation on spirits, on estates, on income, with sixpence in the pound supertax on incomes over five thousand pounds a year. But what created the real furore were the new land duties – taxes on land development, on mineral rights, on land that reverted at the end of a lease and, most striking of all, on the unearned increment of land whose value had been enhanced by the effort of the community in general. It was a direct attack on the profits made by the landowning classes

OPPOSITE The 'People's Budget' introduced by Lloyd George in 1909 brought furious attacks from the landowning classes whose profits were threatened.

from the growth of cities and suburbs. Yet the basic purpose of the budget was financial, to meet an immediate need. Neither local nor central finance could cope with both the old demands on the exchequer and new demands such as old age pensions and the construction of the new 'Dreadnought' battleships. A deficit of sixteen million pounds had somehow to be met, and this was understood. What was really startling about Lloyd George's budget was its political implications. It linked the budget, in the frankest way, with long-term policies of national development, with afforestation, with roads, with public works and urban renewal run by a National Development Commission. It was this, and the clear attempt it implied to wrest the initiative from the House of Lords, which sparked off the crisis. It led to the Upper House committing the supreme folly of rejecting the budget in November 1909 – the first time a finance bill had been rejected for over two hundred and fifty years. Now battle was joined, and on the democratic and social issues of Lloyd George's own choosing. The issue was to be decided, in Lloyd George's vivid phrase, 'before the great assize of the people'.

There is no clear evidence that Lloyd George expected the Lords to reject his budget – their actions severely hamstrung his social policies. But it is equally clear that he seized this new opportunity with the utmost relish. Throughout the prolonged conflict between the Liberal government and the Lords that dragged on until August 1911, when the Parliament Act became law, Lloyd George led the Liberal counter-offensive. He stripped away the false pretensions of the Upper House to be 'the watch-dog of the constitution'. It was, he rejoined, 'Mr Balfour's poodle'. In forceful speeches, notably two at Limehouse (July 1909) and at Newcastle (October 1909), he drew a vivid contrast between the broad social objectives of the government and the selfish financial interests of the peers. They were, he declared, only 'five hundred men chosen at random from among the unemployed', chosen, like a spaniel, on the principle of the 'first of the litter'. The government, by contrast, sought to provide for the 'old workman, finding his way to the tomb, bleeding and footsore, through the brambles and thorns of poverty'. The government's way would lead through 'fields of waving corn'. Alarmed observers compared Lloyd George's attacks with those of Jack Cade, the fifteenth-century rebel. He was depicted in cartoons as a highwaymen or a Welsh poacher. *Punch* showed Lloyd George in the guise of a latter-day John Knox, denouncing 'motorists, golfers and all those miserable

RICH FARE.

The Giant Lloyd-Gorgibuster : " Fee, fi, fo, fat,
I smell the blood of a Plutocrat ;
Be he alive or be he dead,
I'll grind his bones to make my bread."

The famous *Punch* cartoon attacking Lloyd George's budgetary reforms. It depicted Lloyd George as John Knox reviling his congregation from the pulpit for the sins of ownership.

sinners who happen to own anything'. He took a belligerent part in the two general elections held in 1910, in January and December, both of which the Liberals won.

Throughout the tortuous manoeuvres that surrounded the conflict between Asquith's government and the Unionist leaders in the Lords, notably Lord Lansdowne, Lloyd George was foremost among those ministers who urged no surrender. He argued that the power of the Lords to obstruct legislation passed by the Commons, and to harass finance bills, must at all costs be cut back by a suspensory veto and a final ban on their control over money bills. He differed from ministers such as Haldane and Grey who urged instead that the government should reform the composition of the Lords. Lloyd George argued that this would make the parasitical Upper House a rival to the Commons by strengthening its membership: he was, above all, the Great Commoner. Further, he told Masterman that a Lords full of new Liberal peers might be even more hostile to social reform than would Tory backwood squires. He had encountered the narrow social prejudices of *nouveaux-riches* Liberal 'glorified grocers' in Welsh chapels many times in the past. The constitutional crisis was finally resolved in August 1911 after the King's pledge to create peers if the Parliament Bill were not passed was made known. It was a total triumph for the government. Lloyd George's People's Budget had become law; his social programme had been vindicated. He wrote to his wife (11 August 1911) that 'the dream of Liberalism is realised at last'. He and his colleagues had secured an historic triumph. His status as the tribune of popular radicalism had never seemed more secure.

Yet it was at the height of the parliamentary crisis between the government and the peers in the summer of 1910 that Lloyd George's political aspirations followed a totally new course. At the very moment, apparently, when he was spear-

The outstanding figures of the Liberal party were clearly recognised to be Lloyd George and Churchill, here seen triumphantly aloft their tottering prime minister, Asquith.

heading the radical assault on privilege and vested interest, he made a secret proposal to the Unionist leaders for a coalition between the two major parties. The endless distractions of conflict between the Lords and the Commons reinforced his dislike for partisan politics. He suggested, therefore, to Balfour on the Unionist side, and to Grey on the Liberal, that the two parties act together to promote the supreme causes of social reform at home and military preparedness abroad. To promote the former, he urged a massive assault on unemployment, sickness, slum housing and structural poverty. To advance the latter, he floated the possibility of selective service on the Swiss model. Even conscription was not totally ruled out. For a fleeting moment, the scheme attracted surprisingly widespread support. Balfour, weary from years of party conflict, younger Unionist reformers like Steel Maitland, maverick Liberals like Winston Churchill all warmed to the vision of a supreme national executive to promote relevant national objectives. There was also much support for Lloyd George's claim that 'non-controversial issues' could be dealt with incidentally on the basis of non-partisan commissions – even though these included such highly contentious issues as free trade, Irish Home Rule, Lords' reform and Welsh disestablishment.

But the idea of a coalition in 1910, while it appealed to those like Milner who trumpeted the demands for 'national efficiency', never had a chance of succeeding. Quite simply, the roots of party went too deep, as Lloyd George failed to understand. Asquith in the Liberal camp, Austen Chamberlain in the Unionist, the rank-and-file on each side, sensed correctly that the 'non-contentious' issues outlined by Lloyd George were basic to the politics of the day and could not be spirited away by secret formulae in smoke-filled rooms. Party was a permanent reality, even if Lloyd George's outlook as a Welsh outsider made him reluctant to take the point. The dream of a national coalition dissolved and by the end of 1910 Lloyd George had again assumed his familiar posture of belligerent radicalism.

Even so, the vision of a 'sacred union' to promote higher social and political ends did not totally disappear from view. It retained some appeal for younger men like Churchill and F.E. Smith. It had some currency amongst apostles of imperialism close to Milner and detached from the usual party conflict. Among these were men like Philip Kerr, Lionel Curtis and Leopold Amery, all destined to play significant roles in Lloyd George's ministry after 1916. In the vaguest outline, some of the strategy and some of the machinery for a British version of

Theodore Roosevelt's 'New Nationalism' currently canvassed in the United States were given substance. They remained a part of the political scene in Britain even in the vicious party in-fighting of 1911 to 1914. What the coalition episode of 1910 showed was that Lloyd George's version of nationalist-socialism was unacceptable in the normal climate of peacetime politics. But if a world war were to put party politics in abeyance, Lloyd George's vision and his entire role in British politics as a potential leader would be totally transformed.

The years that followed the triumphant passage of the Parliament Bill in August 1911 brought, for the first time, a somewhat less successful phase in Lloyd George's career. After years of extraordinary and almost unbroken political achievement, his progress was interrupted by setbacks. It was a period, though, which began with perhaps his great legislative triumph – the National Insurance Bill of 1911. This was the zenith of Lloyd George's career as a social reformer. It was achieved almost single-handed. No other member of the Cabinet was now identified with welfare measures. Churchill had been soured by labour unrest in the mines and railways; he had moved to the Home Office, and his period as a social reformer was rapidly

Lloyd George's National Insurance Bill of 1911 brought with it fierce opposition, including a country-wide outcry from mistresses and servants against the actual licking of the insurance stamps.

giving way to an instinctive passion for 'law and order'. When he later moved to the Admiralty he and Lloyd George were to be locked in conflict (January 1914) over Churchill's demands for a much higher naval expenditure. Lloyd George's associates now were less powerful men – Sir Rufus Isaacs, the Jewish Attorney-General, and Charles Masterman, a Christian socialist not yet in the Cabinet. Beyond these, he was now friendly with George Riddell, the proprietor of *News of the World*, who bought Lloyd George a new car and a new home at Walton Heath, near his favourite golf course. With limited assistance from his Cabinet colleagues, Lloyd George brought his National Insurance Bill safely through the storms. He faced relentless opposition outside the House. He had to cope with the industrial assurance companies and the friendly societies who ran their own insurance schemes. He faced a disreputable campaign launched by the British Medical Association, neither then nor later sympathetic to social welfare. The trade unions and many socialists were hostile to the idea of insurance being paid for by flat-rate contributions levied directly on working-men, rather than being financed by the central government from general taxation. Finally, there was an extraordinary public campaign mounted by duchesses and their housemaids who attacked bureaucracy and declared that they would never lick stamps for Lloyd George.

With unique dexterity, Lloyd George steered a sure course through all these obstacles. He won over the insurance companies. He detached some of the rank-and-file doctors from the BMA leadership, as another Welsh radical, Aneurin Bevan, was to do thirty-five years later in launching the National Health Service. 'A deputation of doctors,' Lloyd George observed, 'is a deputation of swell doctors': the ordinary GP might have a different attitude. He persuaded most of the Labour MPs in the House to vote for the National Insurance Bill in return for an undertaking that the payment of members would then be introduced. Finally Lloyd George's handling of the complex details of the Insurance Bill in the House was admitted on all sides to be masterly. *Punch* depicted him receiving the acclaim of the stalls as well as of the upper gallery in the political theatre. The result was a decisive stride towards a welfare state. A comprehensive system of national health insurance was set up. There was also a much more limited scheme of unemployment insurance. Lloyd George was less enthusiastic about this part of the bill and had the original proposals watered down, and merged into his own favoured

Sir Rufus Isaacs, Lloyd George and Charles Masterman at Criccieth in 1911.

scheme of health insurance. Benefits were to be paid as of right to all insured persons, which broke away from the unjust traditions of the old Poor Law based on 'less eligibility'. At the same time, the idea of insurance made the scheme financially respectable, while Lloyd George left room for thrift and private effort as Victorian morality demanded. A compromise had been worked out between a thorough-going collectivism and the tenets of private enterprise. Another, less regarded, feature of the Act was the provision for medical research, in which Lloyd George, aware of such problems as tuberculosis in Wales, was much interested. Finally, new machinery was created for the state provision of welfare, through the new insurance commissions. Men like Sir Arthur Salter and Thomas Jones, major figures in central government a few years later, made their entry into the corridors of power for the first time. The civil service was massively underpinned. And this whole revolution went through without a party revolt, without much

Vandyk

protest from even the most backward-looking of Liberal 'glorified grocers'. Even though the Insurance Act at first lost the Liberals votes in by-elections in 1912 to 1913, Asquith backed up his Chancellor throughout. Even a jaundiced critic like Beatrice Webb paid tribute to Lloyd George's 'heroic demagoguery' and acknowledged it as his most brilliant achievement.

Despite this triumph, however, the next few years brought a darker period in his life. There were personal problems which contributed here. In 1912 there entered permanently into his life Miss Frances Stevenson, a Wimbledon school-teacher originally hired as a French tutor for Megan. She became his intimate confidante and private secretary, and in 1943 she became Lloyd George's second wife. She noted in her memoirs that 'their real marriage' had taken place thirty years earlier. The gulf that had developed between Lloyd George and his wife since the death of Mair in 1907, Mrs Lloyd George's steadfast refusal to live in London for any length of time – these facts finally reaped their harvest.

There were money troubles also. Lloyd George had always tended to be careless about money matters, though never corrupt. The Andes gold mining venture in Patagonia in the 1890s was testimony to this. In the summer of 1912 it came out that he and the Attorney-General, Rufus Isaacs, had misguidedly bought shares in the American Marconi Company at a time when the British Marconi Company was about to enter into a highly profitable contract with the British government to build wireless telegraphy stations throughout the empire. Acting on advice from Godfrey Isaacs, the Attorney-General's brother, and a director of the American Marconi Company, Lloyd George bought first a thousand and later a further three thousand Marconi shares. In fact, he lost money on the deal (whereas Rufus Isaacs made a substantial profit). Even so, there was a clear suspicion that ministers of the Crown had used their public knowledge of state decisions to line their own pockets. 'Marconi' continued to plague the government, and Lloyd George in particular, from the summer of 1912 to the spring of the following year; the role played by wireless in reporting the sinking of the *Titanic* added to the drama of the affair. Anti-semitism was also stirred up in the gutter press against the 'two Hebrews' involved, while Northcliffe in the *Daily Mail* seized the chance to attack the 'Welsh solicitor and the Jew barrister', two of the great outsiders of public life. Lloyd George was the main target. He offered Asquith his

OPPOSITE Frances Stevenson who became Lloyd George's private secretary in 1912 and shortly afterwards his mistress. She eventually became Lloyd George's second wife in 1943.

OPPOSITE The Marconi scandal did much to damage Lloyd George's reputation and the official clearing of blame was widely accused of being a sham.

resignation, and only the decision of the government to fight the issue out on a strictly partisan basis and to support a white-washing committee report on the affair saved him. Balfour not unfairly commented that the word 'regret' did not figure prominently in Lloyd George's explanations. He had been careless rather than dishonest, but it seriously undermined his public reputation at a critical time.

Private problems were accompanied by political setbacks. Lloyd George's attempt to restore his and the government's credit by a new land campaign in the autumn of 1913 fell rather flat. Even programmes as radical as publicly-supported housing schemes and the taxing of site values failed to capture the public imagination, and Lloyd George knew it. Perhaps the rural radicalism of his youth was losing its magic in an urbanised society. At all events, it was a crusade that went wrong. In addition, he failed in his battle with Churchill over the 1914 naval estimates, and again contemplated resignation. The 1914 budget was another near-failure. It was an important budget, more radical than that of 1909, with a supertax, and the first introduction of graduated income tax on earned incomes. But it proved to be a parliamentary fiasco. There were serious procedural difficulties with the Speaker, who ruled that the budget was not a 'money bill' as defined by the Parliament Act of 1911. So another of Lloyd George's radical moves failed to gain real momentum. Charles Masterman described him in May 1914 (writing to Sir Arthur Ponsonby) as 'jumpy, irritable, overworked and unhappy'. Lloyd George seemed increasingly isolated now. In the Cabinet he had no close associates – oddly enough, Grey was in some ways the closest. Right-wingers like Runciman and McKenna (a bitter foe of Lloyd George from now on) were relentlessly hostile. Nor was he close to the radical backbenchers or to his own Welsh Party. Only in some sections of the national and local newspaper press did he retain his earlier clear support.

Of course, his political decline at this time should not be exaggerated. He was still indispensable to Asquith, since he was still the main voice of popular radicalism in the government. He was still a vital link with organised labour, with a rare skill in labour negotiations such as in settling the railway strike of August 1911. He was also active in trying to break the deadlock over Ireland. In early 1914 he outlined a plan which would temporarily suspend the application of the Irish Home Rule Bill to Ulster (or, at least, the six north-eastern counties of it) for a period of years. This confirmed the qualifications that must

BLAMELESS TELEGRAPHY.

John Bull. "My boys, you leave the court without a stain—except, perhaps, for the whitewash."

be placed in assessing Lloyd George as a Home Ruler. In this sense, he was still a disciple of Joseph Chamberlain. Nevertheless, the conclusion must remain that Lloyd George was comparatively in the shadows in the period after 1911. His reputation was not quite at the same high level, especially in radical circles, that it had been three years earlier.

Then, on 4 August 1914, Lloyd George's career was completely transformed. War broke out in Europe and Britain declared war on Germany. Up till now, he had taken only an occasional interest in foreign affairs, despite the broadening outlook induced by the Boer War. He was almost wholly associated in the public mind with domestic issues. Even so, since his famous

TADDY'S MYRTLE GROVE CIGARETTES (MEDIUM) 10 for 3D. Sold by all licensed dealers in Tobacco

The Evening News

London's Predominant Evening Journal. Largest Net Sale in the United Kingdom.

NO. 10,216. [Thirty-Third Year.] LONDON: TUESDAY, AUGUST 4, 1914. ONE

BRITISH ULTIMATUM TO GERMANY.

TO REPLY BY MIDNIGHT.

The Unsatisfactory Answers of Germany.

BELGIUM'S APPEAL.

In the House of Commons this afternoon Mr. Asquith announced the despatch by Britain of an ultimatum to Germany.

MR. ASQUITH SAID A TELEGRAM WAS SENT THIS MORNING BY SIR E. GREY TO THE BRITISH AMBASSADOR AT BERLIN INFORMING HIM OF THE APPEAL MADE BY THE KING OF THE BELGIANS FOR DIPLOMATIC INTERVENTION.

BELGIUM HAD CATEGORICALLY REFUSED TO SANCTION A FLAGRANT VIOLATION OF THE LAW OF NATIONS.

THE GERMAN GOVERNMENT HAS BEEN ASKED TO GIVE A SATISFACTORY REPLY BY MIDNIGHT ON THE QUESTION OF BELGIAN NEUTRALITY.

THE BRITISH GOVERNMENT HAD REQUESTED AN ASSURANCE THAT THE NEUTRALITY OF BELGIUM WOULD BE RESPECTED BY GERMANY

SUMMARY OF TO-DAY'S WAR NEWS.

It is reported, but not confirmed, that German and French warships have fought off Flamborough Head.

Germany is stated to have declared that if she considers it essential she will break through Belgian territory by force of arms.

German troops are said to have invaded Belgium.

A German company is reported to have reached Mars-la-Tour.

The British Government have been informed officially that German troops are in Belgium. At noon to-day the German Embassy issued a statement that no troops had crossed the frontier.

A correspondent says that Belgium may interrupt German communications by flooding the country on their invasion route.

The Commander-in-Chief of the French Army is on his way to the frontier.

The Cabinet sat from 11.30 to 1.35 p.m.

Lord Haldane is taking over Mr. Asquith's duties as Secretary of State for War till the Cabinet can find a way of relieving him.

It is reported that Lord Morley has resigned from the Cabinet. Mr. John Burns, it is said, also may resign.

The Cabinet is expected to take action that will prevent food gambling and fix the price of bread.

Lord Roberts and Sir John French visited the War Office.

The Army Reserves are called up and the Territorial Force is to be embodied.

The British Army is being mobilised.

Australia offers us 20,000 men.

A German liner with £2,000,000 in specie has put into Falmouth.

The Turkish Army is mobilising.

THE BULLYING OF BELGIUM.

Germany Prepared to Carry Through "Essential Measures" by Force of Arms.

AEROPLANE BOMBS.

FRENCH FRONTIER TOWN DAMAGED.

TURKEY THE LATEST POWER TO MOBILISE.

TO-DAY'S CABLES.

PARIS, Tuesday.

Shortly before six o'clock yesterday evening, a German aeroplane dropped three bombs in the town of Luneville. Some damage was done, but there were no casualties.—Reuter.

PARIS, Tuesday.

A German airman this morning dropped three bombs over Luneville from a height of 4,500 feet, doing material damage only.

(Lunéville, a manufacturing town about sixteen miles south-east of Nancy, came into prominence some time ago owing to the inadvertent

The River Barrage at Vise which is to be destroyed by the Belgians with the object of flooding the country between Liege and Verviers to delay the German advance.

GERMAN GOLD-SHIP AT FALMOUTH.

£2,000,000 SPECIE FOR LONDON AND PARIS.

The Evening News understands that the North German Lloyd steamship Kronprinzessin Cecilie, bound from New York to Bremen with £2,000,000 in specie aboard, put into Falmouth, Cornwall, early to-day.

It is not yet known whether she will remain there until hostilities are over.

It is stated that the specie is consigned to London and Paris.

The Kronprinzessin Cecilie (a vessel of 19,500 tons) is the boat which was signalled from Malin Head, on the north-west coast of Ireland, on Sunday.

From this it was supposed that she was making for Germany direct by the north of Scotland.

THE CITY'S ANXIETY.

While recognising the delicate international questions involved at the present moment, financial people are inclined to view with satisfaction the presence of this treasure in an English harbour.

Even if its diversion to the vaults of the Bank of England should not prove permissible, its non-arrival in Germany is all to the good, because its delivery there would mean an addition to German financial resources for the prosecution of the war.

GERMANY'S LATEST.

CRUISER BOMBARDS A PORT ON THE ALGERIAN COAST.

A message from the French Embassy in

TURKEY MOBILISING.

A GERMAN GENERAL TO TAKE COMMAND.

Europe's adversity is Turkey's opportunity, and no one will be surprised by the news to-day that she is mobilising.

The important fact that the Ottoman army will be under the command of General Liman von Sanders, chief of the German military mission in Turkey, is added by Reuter's Agency.

The agency has also received the following:—

"The Ottoman Consulate-General beg to inform the Ottoman Reservists living in Great Britain that the general mobilisation of the Imperial Ottoman Army and Navy having been ordered—with the exception of the 7th Army Corps and the independent 22nd and 23rd divisions—the Ottoman Reservists can apply to the Turkish Consulate-General, 7, Union-court, Old Broad-street, London, E.C., for full particulars."

The approximate peace strength of the Turkish Army is about 230,000 of all arms and ranks. Since 1909 the organisation and training of the army has been under the direction of the German Military Mission of which the new generalissimo is the head.

The Turkish Navy consists of two Dreadnoughts, three old battleships, one of which was launched in 1874, two cruisers, two torpedo gunboats, and a variety of small gunboats, eight destroyers, and nine torpedo boats.

There are 30,000 sailors and about 9,000 marines.

The Navy has been in the course of reorganisation since 1909 under a British Admiral and a British staff of navigating, torpedo, and gunnery officers.

visit to Germany in the summer of 1908, he had been increasingly preoccupied with the worsening international situation. During that visit, he had held discussions with the German chancellor, Bethmann Hollwegg, about Anglo-German naval rivalry. Perhaps he meditated playing the kind of conciliatory role in international politics that he had frequently done in English and Welsh politics in the past. He was plainly no pacifist and no isolationist. His memorandum on a coalition government in August 1910 had even mentioned conscription, at that time taboo to all right-thinking Liberals. In July 1911 he startled the public with a speech at the Mansion House in which he seemed to threaten Germany with military retaliation as a result of its provocative stand in the Agadir crisis in Morocco. The precise significance of this speech is not clear but the prevailing view amongst historians is that it was directed against Germany. 'I am not going to be jack-booted by anyone,' commented Lloyd George to Riddell. He and Churchill were said by Sir Arthur Nicolson (17 August 1911) 'to be a little disappointed that war did not occur'. From that summer Lloyd George was a member of the Committee of Imperial Defence and thus in close touch with British strategic and defence plans. He again moved closer to Grey, the Foreign Secretary. He was never a peacemonger either in public or in private. However, to most commentators he was still placed in the 'peace party' of the Cabinet. After all, he repeatedly spoke of the need for a more tranquil international climate. He argued against escalating expenditure on the army and the navy. As late as 9 July 1914, after the murder of the Austrian Archduke, Franz Ferdinand, at Sarajevo, he told an audience at the Guildhall that 'the sky has never been more perfectly blue'.

Even so, in the supreme crisis of 30 July to 4 August 1914 Lloyd George moved, with seeming inevitability, towards an acceptance of war. No account of these anxious days can do justice to his position unless it stresses the agony of conscience that he went through. Until 2 August he was amongst those who strove to minimise the British territorial commitment to France. Nevertheless he had long anticipated that a German invasion of Belgium was probable, and that Britain would then inevitably have to intervene, even if only to keep the sea lanes open in the first instance. He viewed the onset of war with blank terror – 'I am filled with horror at the prospect,' he wrote to his wife on 3 August. He detested the idea of Britain's becoming embroiled in an open-ended land war in Europe, especially if it meant an alliance with Czarist Russia. Still, in the ultimate

Part of newspaper front page for 4 August 1914.

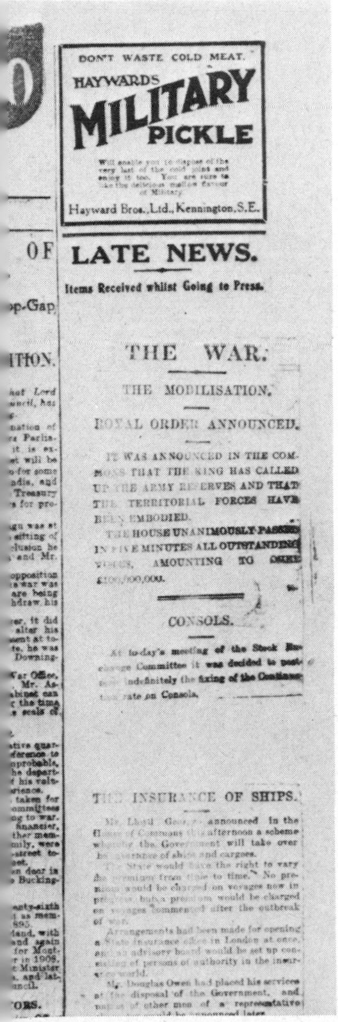

LATE NEWS.

Items Received whilst Going to Press.

THE WAR.

THE MOBILISATION.

ROYAL ORDER ANNOUNCED.

IT WAS ANNOUNCED IN THE COMMONS THAT THE KING HAS CALLED UP THE ARMY RESERVES AND THAT THE TERRITORIAL FORCES HAVE BEEN EMBODIED.

THE HOUSE UNANIMOUSLY PASSED IN FIVE MINUTES ALL OUTSTANDING VOTES, AMOUNTING TO OVER £100,000,000.

CONSOLS.

At to-day's meeting of the Stock Exchange Committee it was decided to postpone indefinitely the fixing of the Continuation rate on Consols.

THE INSURANCE OF SHIPS.

Mr. Lloyd George announced in the House of Commons this afternoon a scheme whereby the Government will take over the insurance of ships and cargoes.

The State would have the right to vary the premium from time to time. No premium would be charged on voyages now in progress, but a premium would be charged on voyages commenced after the outbreak of war.

Arrangements had been made for opening a State insurance office in London at once, and an advisory board would be set up consisting of persons of authority in the insurance world.

Mr. Douglas Owen had placed his services at the disposal of the Government, and names of other men of a representative [illegible] analysis, there was never any prospect of his joining Morley, Burns and Trevelyan in resignation from the government. He had had little contact with peace-minded backbenchers like Ponsonby or Morrell, however much he might have inspired them in the past. The wilderness had little appeal for him now, even in a Welsh oasis. After a moment of doubt on 3 August, he committed himself finally and decisively to war. Unwittingly he had also taken the decisive moral commitment that would lead him to the premiership.

Freed from the indecision of the pre-war days, Lloyd George at once found a new buoyancy and hope in the challenge of wartime. At last the party truce that he had sometimes visualised in the past had come about. By the end of September, even such controversial domestic issues as Irish Home Rule and Welsh disestablishment had been placed in suspended animation until the war came to an end. His first notable achievements now came at the Treasury. He reacted with vigour and confidence in dealing with the immediate monetary crisis after 4 August. He acted with Lord Cunliffe, the governor of the Bank of England; he restored confidence among the 'flapping penguins' of the city; he impressed even Keynes by his vitality and nerve. By 10 August the financial emergency was over, and the bank moratorium ended. New one pound and ten shilling treasury notes were issued to swell the fiduciary issue of the banks – specimens of these were faithfully dispatched to the Lloyd George children in Criccieth. Specie payments and the gold standard were maintained. Bank rate came down. On all sides, economists, long suspicious of Lloyd George's astuteness in money matters, now sang the praises of his grasp of the principles of public finance. His first wartime budget in November 1914, though open to attack for its unwillingness to increase direct taxation, again enhanced his glowing reputation as a departmental chief, at a time when most other ministers were being severely criticised.

Until mid-September, however, he had been little enough involved with the course of the war. There was some speculation that his commitment to total war was perhaps less wholehearted than that of other ministers. These speculations were totally dispelled on 19 September by a stirring recruiting speech made to a large audience of London Welshmen at the Queen's Hall, one which had taken weeks to prepare. In substance his speech was conventional enough, with sentimental reference to Wales, Belgium, Serbia and other 'five-foot-five nations'. What was unfamiliar was his uninhibited commitment to all-out war,

Men queuing up to enlist at Southwark Town Hall.

his strident nationalism, his jingo assaults on Germany as 'the road hog of Europe', his pledge that the allies would advance 'from terror to triumph'. Floods of letters of support that poured into Frances Stevenson's office confirmed that he was gaining a new national stature. Further recruiting speeches later in the autumn reinforced his new reputation across the country.

These speeches gained him new respect amongst the Unionists and the right wing. In addition, he was also building up anew his contacts with organised labour. It was he who was almost solely responsible, the following March, for negotiating the so-called 'treasury agreement'. Here he managed to secure the agreement of the trade unions to the 'dilution' of the work force by unskilled workers (including women) and to a suspension of strikes. In return he offered a vague promise to check wartime profiteering, and a firmer pledge to protect collective bargaining. His standing with the unions had never stood higher, at a time when he was winning new admirers amongst industrialists and businessmen.

Among his own Liberals, his reputation was less certain. Many of his old radical friends felt uneasy at his nationalistic belligerence, his lack of concern with civil liberties and the old Liberal values. Even conscription seemed no longer unthinkable. Of his recent Liberal colleagues, Rufus Isaacs had been removed to the bench as Lord Chief Justice (a singularly curious appointment after the irregularities of the Marconi affair). Lloyd George had quarrelled violently with Charles Masterman after disagreement over a by-election nomination in Swansea. More than ever within Liberal ranks, Lloyd George was alone. Many Liberals, headed by McKenna, showed open dislike of their pushing Welsh colleague; Asquith recorded McKenna and Lloyd George as 'fighting like fishwives' in full Cabinet. Still, even amongst Liberals, Lloyd George could claim that he provided an example of Liberals governing with efficiency, and without the sacrifice of humanitarian considerations. It was not surprising that the *Daily Chronicle* and other Liberal journals began to publish unsupported rumours that he might aim higher than number 11 Downing Street.

The outstanding feature of Lloyd George's political outlook in early 1915 was his mounting disillusion with the conduct of the war by Asquith's government. From 1 January, he advanced searching criticism of the conduct of military policy on the western front. He demanded 'a definite victory somewhere'. He condemned the policy of bloody stalemate in the trenches in France, and urged a more flexible strategy of assaults on the rear of the German and Austrian positions by new invasions in the Balkans, perhaps in Serbia. He was amongst those who had approved of the expedition to the Dardanelles, though Churchill alone was left bearing the brunt of public condemnation when the expedition collapsed in bloody failure. Lloyd George was also a fierce critic of the supply of munitions and played his part in whipping up national concern at the supposed shortage of shells for which the War Minister, Lord Kitchener, was given the blame. Over the whole range of policies, Asquith's government was now in total disarray. Lloyd George himself contributed to this by advancing, for reasons that are still obscure, a scheme for dealing with the drink issue by the nationalisation of all public houses. The only results were a

OPPOSITE Asquith, Liberal prime minister, whose position was fundamentally affected by the formation of the first coalition in May 1915.

pilot scheme of state 'pubs' at Carlisle, and the observance of 'the King's Pledge' of total abstinence by the unfortunate George v – and by him alone! This issue still further undermined the Cabinet, already gripped by acute doubt and dissension.

Still there is no evidence that Lloyd George was actively disloyal to Asquith. The crisis of 17 to 24 May 1915, which saw the government suddenly turned into a national coalition still under Asquith's leadership, was in no way generated by Lloyd George. The root cause was the Unionists' inability to continue the party truce, and Asquith's passionate desire to maintain his own leadership after the outcry caused by the supposed shortage of shells had put his premiership in some peril. Although Lloyd George's private meeting with Bonar Law on 17 May helped to bring the crisis to a head, he was not in any sense the main agent of it. On the other hand, with but Lloyd George's support, Asquith could not have survived – at one point Lloyd George even turned down Law's offer of the premiership. Asquith could sacrifice Haldane, an old friend now cast aside in the face of crude anti-German sentiment, but Lloyd George was crucial to the ministry's survival. In the event, Lloyd George's decisions reinforced Asquith's position

Contemporary postcard acknowledging Lloyd George's immediate effectiveness as Minister of Munitions.

as premier. He helped to persuade Bonar Law not to take the Treasury but to go to the humbler post of Colonial Secretary. He then allowed his bitter foe, McKenna, to go to the Treasury on a temporary basis. Finally, he agreed, with much reluctance, to move from the Treasury (though he stayed on at 11 Downing Street) to the unknown trials of the new Ministry of Munitions. Asquith himself was almost overcome with gratitude to Lloyd George for enabling him to retain the levers of power. Margot Asquith herself, often a vicious critic of the 'Welsh wizard', now wrote (26 May): 'L.G. has come grandly out of this – he has the sweetest nature in the world.'

Sir Edward Carson, Irish leader of the Unionist backbenchers, and an ardent conscriptionist.

Lloyd George's period as Minister of Munitions from May 1915 to July 1916 can be seen in retrospect as a vital phase in his rise to the premiership. Few suspected this at the time. Indeed, there was little coherent discussion during this period of his possible supplanting of Asquith at any stage. In the first place, Lloyd George's period at Munitions was a new dramatic demonstration of his executive genius. The decisive moves were made in the transition to an economy geared to total war. New controls were imposed on the supply and allocation of raw materials. Men of 'push and go' carried out the minister's demands. Supplementary advisers were also found, for instance Professor Chaim Weizmann, who showed how acetone could be made from horse-chestnuts. Conditions for men working in government munitions factories were also transformed, and acted as a pace-setter for private industry. Women worked in industrial employment, with profound results for their social status.

More interest perhaps attaches to the way in which the years at the Munitions Ministry broadened still further Lloyd George's political appeal. His relations with the trade unions were improved by his new concern for welfare conditions in government factories. Through his parliamentary secretary, Arthur Lee, he built up contacts with Lord Milner and his imperialist 'Round Table' followers: among these was Philip Kerr, later to be his most intimate adviser. He also forged a new relationship with the Irish Unionist leader, Sir Edward Carson, which was shortly to benefit them both. However, with the orthodox Unionist leaders – men like Law, Austen Chamberlain and Walter Long – Lloyd George preserved relatively frigid relations. They still regarded him as essentially the voice of left-wing radicalism, and they were correct.

By contrast, his year at Munitions added new strains to his relations with his fellow Liberals. His new concern with

Some of the casualties of the Somme offensive, July 1916, in which the British army was cut to pieces.

national arms and manpower resources turned his mind again to a gloomy contemplation of the conduct of the war. To him, as to many others, Asquith, saddened by the death of a son, partially befuddled by brandy, was now tired and indecisive, no longer the dominating leader he had been in times of peace. The War Cabinet was leisurely and inefficient. Vital information never reached it, while effective direction was seldom imposed either on Sir John French (commander on the western front) or on his successor, Sir Douglas Haig, whom Lloyd George much disliked. In the winter of 1915 to 1916, disaster followed disaster – a severe setback at Loos, the collapse of the Dardanelles expedition, the bleeding white of the French army at Verdun. There were one hundred and forty-two thousand British casualties in four days' fighting at Arras. The bloody climax came in July 1916 with the cutting to pieces of the British army in the Somme offensive. Haig lost sixty thousand men on 1 July, the first day, twenty thousand of them killed. The British and French army now vied in pursuing inhuman battering-ram tactics in the vain pursuit of the mirage of national honour. Lloyd George's discontent was unexpectedly exposed to the House of Commons in a speech on 20 December 1915: 'Too late in moving here! Too late in arriving there! . . .

In this war the footsteps of the Allied forces have been dogged by the mocking spectre of "Too late"!'

He needed an issue to focus his criticisms of the government's conduct of the war. He found it in military conscription. The arguments over this question between September 1915 and May 1916 are crucial to an understanding of his political evolution. They go far towards explaining the later split in the Liberal Party. Lloyd George had become convinced of the need for a new political lead. He was increasingly distant towards Asquith. He established new links with Unionist advocates of conscription, men like Curzon, Long, Lansdowne and Carson. Lord Riddell noted in his diary how his closest associates now were Unionists, not Liberals. 'He has completely changed.' The old Liberal values were being eroded by 'strong government'. In pursuit of the 'knock-out blow', civil liberties, peace, retrenchment and reform, the hallowed principles of Gladstone, Cobden and Bright, were being discarded. Speculations in the press about Lloyd George's views on conscription mounted on 13 September 1915 when there was printed, in advance of official publication, the preface to a collection of his war speeches, *From Terror to Triumph*. While it did not openly advocate conscription, it was strongly compulsionist in tone. If everything were sacrificed for the native land, 'then victory is assured'.

Liberals everywhere were startled by this document. Throughout October, November and December, Lloyd George was locked in conflict with Asquith who failed to make a decisive commitment in favour of conscription. He argued, indeed correctly, that voluntary recruitment would supply enough men to meet all current needs. Lloyd George offered his resignation in November, with the hidden threat that the Lords might be used to force through conscription by refusing to prolong the life of the parliament beyond January 1916. On 29 December 1915, Asquith wearily conceded the main point – the conscription of all single men between the ages of eighteen and forty-five. In the ensuing crisis, only Sir John Simon among the Liberal ministers submitted his resignation. Only a handful of minor backbenchers on the Liberal side voted against the government's measure in the House. But the conscription issue continued to simmer and to drive further wedges between Lloyd George and Asquith. In April 1916 Lloyd George was again near to resignation, with several Unionists backing him up. Helplessly, on 20 April Asquith conceded universal male conscription, for married men as well. Lord Riddell noted in his diary, 'The political crisis is over.' But it was overcome at appalling cost to the government's credibility and to Asquith's waning reputation.

Many writers have seen in these prolonged manoeuvres over conscription a 'bid for power' by Lloyd George. There is every evidence that he wanted power to prosecute the war more vigorously. There is none that he was scheming to gain the premiership. In fact, his political position was weak. Among the ranks of labour, his bellicose public speeches were helping to undermine his reputation as the workers' friend. Unionists, however much they might support him over conscription, were still endlessly suspicious of his extra-party manoeuvres and his links with the press. His action to help wind up the Dardanelles expedition, a correct decision on military and on humane grounds, incensed Lord Curzon, while with Bonar Law his relations were still distant. If Lloyd George was credibly to sustain a thrust for national leadership it could only be through the medium of the Liberals. Here he was largely alone. The Liberal War Committee, formed during the conscription crisis as a 'ginger group' to promote a more active prosecution of the war, was a small and relatively uninfluential group of perhaps forty backbenchers. Admittedly it did include men like Sir Alfred Mond, Captain Freddie Guest and 'Bronco Bill' Sutherland who were actively associated with Lloyd George after 1916, but at the time the Committee's importance was symbolic and its membership restricted. After April 1916 it hardly counted. The great mass of rank-and-file Liberals in parliament and the country felt intense loyalty to Asquith, their leader for over eight years. This was reinforced by widespread sympathy for the buffetings he had had to endure during the conscription crises: Frances Stevenson's private diary vastly exaggerates Lloyd George's support in Liberal circles at this time. Far from the conscription issue helping him to form a 'party within a party', it had largely undermined his effective influence over the party in which he had spent his political life. At the start of June 1916, he was again acutely despondent, gloomily contemplating new military disasters, lamenting his inability to reconstruct the government's strategy on positive lines. Again, as Riddell noted, he was near to resignation.

Then came another dramatic shift. Kitchener was drowned at sea on a mission to Russia and Lloyd George was offered by Asquith the vacant post as Secretary for War. After a month's hesitation, Lloyd George finally took the office on 4 July. Far from this involving him more vigorously in the prosecution of the war, however, its immediate consequence was to immerse him again in the dreary bog of Irish Home Rule. Asquith asked him to try to resolve the worsening situation in Ireland, newly inflamed after the Easter rising, and the execution of the Irish republican leaders. Reluctantly, he agreed to do so, and to try to achieve a permanent political settlement. For three weeks he seemed on the edge of an astonishing triumph. Carson, for the Unionists, Redmond, the Nationalist leader, were both persuaded to draft terms for an Irish settlement. Friendly Irish newspapermen like T. P. O'Connor were also drawn in. Remarkable progress was made: in particular the southern Unionists were largely surrendered, with Carson's agreement. But it was the usual obstacle of Protestant Ulster which frustrated Lloyd George's designs. Was the exclusion of the six Protestant counties to be temporary or permanent? Nobody knew, and the vehement criticisms of Unionist ministers such as Walter Long and Lord Lansdowne soon undermined the

Cartoon from the *Western Mail* of Lloyd George 'ready for his new part' as Secretary for War.

Wreckage in Dublin following the Easter Week rising in 1916.

bipartisan unity that surrounded the talks. By the end of July Lloyd George admitted failure, his disillusion with Asquith and orthodox party politics more evident than ever. In so far as his manoeuvres had alienated Irish Nationalists like John Dillon and newly antagonised Unionists like Walter Long, Lloyd George had finished up more isolated and distrusted. In the autumn of 1916 his pessimism became more and more pronounced. There were setbacks almost everywhere, culminating in the failure to aid Rumania, another 'five-foot-five nation'. Speculation about Lloyd George's future continued to build up in the daily press. Only his proven ability in supreme office, unmatched by any other politician of the day, kept him in the government. In despair, he told Hankey, secretary of the War Committee, on 9 November, 'We are going to lose this war.'

Between 20 November and 9 December 1916 these doubts and tensions were resolved by a complex train of events which remain to this day acutely controversial. In mid-November, Bonar Law sensed a threat to his leadership from the Unionist backbenches. From 20 November, through the mediation of the mercurial Canadian newspaperman, Max Aitken (later Lord Beaverbrook), he began negotiations with Lloyd George and Carson about remodelling the government. They sent a draft to Asquith on 1 December which was effectively rejected. Lloyd George then rallied Bonar Law with a famous note, 'The life of the country depends on resolute action by you *now*.' On 3 December Asquith did accept a revised scheme, one still acceptable to Lloyd George. It would set up a supreme War Committee of three men, but would retain Asquith as prime minister. The crisis appeared to be over. Quite unexpectedly, Asquith threw out the agreement early on Monday, 4 December. In the next thirty-six hours he lost the Unionist support which he had previously retained. Lloyd George submitted his resignation, and Bonar Law followed him. Unable to continue in office, unwilling to serve under any other leader, Asquith surrendered the seals of office on 5 December. Bonar Law predictably declined the offer of the premiership, and by the evening of 7 December Lloyd George had kissed hands as prime minister. In the next two days he was able to form the basis of an all-party government. By 9 December he was both secure in Unionist support and had won over the Labour Party. Most spectacular of all, over a hundred Liberal backbenchers, none of them of major stature, had endorsed his leadership. At the head of this patchwork administration, at a critical time in the war, Lloyd George took over as prime minister.

Behind this brief narrative lies a complex skein of political imponderables. No aspect of his career has done more to cloud Lloyd George's reputation than the events of the first week of December 1916. It has often been alleged that he gained power through a sordid conspiracy with the Unionists, with the aid of Northcliffe and other press lords, and that Asquith was the honourable and hapless victim of treachery. Lloyd George is portrayed as 'the envious Casca', Asquith as 'the noblest Roman of them all'. But, now that we have the advantage of an immense range of new material, including latterly the papers of Lord Beaverbrook, a very different version of these critical events can be put forward.

First of all, the discussions between Lloyd George, Bonar Law and Carson were no conspiracy: Asquith was kept fully informed about them from 20 November onwards. Secondly, there is no evidence, direct or indirect, that Lloyd George was trying to build up an anti-Asquith faction within the Liberal Party, or that he thought of doing so. It was only after he took on the premiership on 7 December that Addison, David Davies and other Liberal backbenchers tried to rally Liberal support behind him. Thirdly, it was Asquith, not Lloyd George, who broke off negotiations. He threw over the agreed draft prepared by Hankey and Montagu on the basis of Lloyd George's earlier proposals, giving a leading article in *The Times* as a flimsy excuse. Further, Asquith broke off discussions in a way that clearly sounded the call to battle. As A.J.P. Taylor has written: 'The compromise with Lloyd George made him perfectly safe and he deliberately went back on it.' Why Asquith acted in so rash a manner is still mysterious, though it seems that it was very much his own private decision to do so. Fourthly, it was only after this event that it was at all possible for Lloyd George to amass the wide-ranging political support he needed to become Prime Minister of a coalition government. Asquith's behaviour, plus the wavering of the other Unionist leaders, made the links between Bonar Law and Lloyd George an unshakable alliance. In the face of this, with Bonar Law showing a tenacity and courage that few had suspected, Curzon, Long and the other Unionists could not continue in office, and Asquith had to resign. The general conclusion must be that it was Asquith's erratic behaviour, not Lloyd George's intrigues, which eroded the government. In the final crisis, even Sir Edward Grey, an aloof Liberal patrician, was impressed by the contrast between Lloyd George's decisiveness and Asquith's dithering. Asquith had finally to make a desperate bid to rally support, detaching Lloyd George and Bonar Law but retaining his other ministers. This time he made the same mistake that Lloyd George had made in 1910 when he advocated a coalition – Asquith, of all people, underestimated the strength of a party leader. He failed to give serious attention to Bonar Law's crucial position and this proved to be a fatal miscalculation. Lloyd George then kissed hands as prime minister on the evening of 7 December, having won over the Labour Party leaders earlier that day. 'I think I shall be Prime Minister before 7 o'clock,' he told Frances Stevenson that afternoon. So he was.

Interpreting Lloyd George's bewildering changes of role in the years between the end of the South African War and his emergence as premier is peculiarly difficult. The changes appear to be so abrupt. There seems, at first sight, to be a complete transformation from a left-wing radical of little Englander outlook in 1902 to a nationalist/state socialist in 1916 with a sympathy for empire. In the years between, the Old Liberalism of free trade and the chapel vote, the New Liberalism of pensions and insurance, issues like land reform which straddled them both, came and went. Yet there are elements of continuity throughout this period. Lloyd George was never a traditional Liberal even in the heady days of 1906. He was always

OPPOSITE Lloyd George in his new role of prime minister. He succeeded Asquith on 7 December 1916.

THE NEW CONDUCTOR.

OPENING OF THE 1917 OVERTURE.

enthusiastic for strong government; unlike most radicals, he had no fear of power. Nor was he a little Englander, still less a pacifist, after 1902. He had a powerful instinct for what he conceived to be the national interest. It was entirely consistent that he should become the major advocate of 'all-out war' and 'the knock-out blow' after 1914. Finally, even in 1902 his casual attitude to the world of party politics was discernible. He had shown a willingness to bypass orthodox party alignments during the Welsh county council 'revolt'. He had been prepared to negotiate in an open-ended way with industrialists and trade union leaders at the Board of Trade. He had totally transformed the range of Liberal policies while at the Treasury, using the widest basis of support, in parliament, the civil service, in industry and in Fleet Street. All these suggest links between the Welsh sharpshooter of 1902 and the apostle of strong central government who took office as premier in December 1916.

But ultimately it was the pressure of events which shaped his career. It was war that made Lloyd George prime minister, as it later made Churchill. Total war required a new supreme command which could provide continuity between the radical reforms of 1906 to 1914 and the new pressures of wartime society. Asquith and the orthodox Liberals – the McKennas and the Runcimans – were unable to supply this: perhaps this is a comment on their basic decency. Lloyd George seemed uniquely capable of bridging the gap. He alone had the adaptability, the flair, the creativity, the toughness to provide a new style of premiership. Perhaps only the Welsh outsider, detached from the conventional party scene, could have fulfilled this role in 1916, as Churchill, another outsider, was to do in 1940. Lord Beaverbrook has left a moving account of this moment. Calling on Lloyd George as he moved into 10 Downing Street, he observed how a momentary nervous exhaustion gave way to a new surge of courage. From now on, he wrote, Lloyd George would be 'the idol of the nation', the most powerful prime minister in history. He would 'dictate to Europe, fling out a great dynasty with a gesture and parcel out the frontiers of races. . . . There, in this entry of his new day of glory, with the faded pictures of his predecessors on the walls around him, sits David Lloyd George, Premier of Great Britain.'

4

LEADER IN WAR
1916-18

Lloyd George's war premiership was without parallel in British history. No previous prime minister had ever exercised power in so sweeping and dominating a manner. The style and significance of his years of ascendancy provoked anxious comment at the time; they have led to endless controversy amongst historians and political scientists ever since. Yet nothing seemed less probable in the second week of December 1916 than that Lloyd George should occupy the supreme office – 'the driver's seat' as Beaverbrook was to describe it – in so emphatic a way. At first, his basic problem was one of simple survival. He was a prime minister without a party. The vast bulk of Liberals in the Commons were either equivocal or hostile, and he depended on the tender mercies of the Unionists, for long his bitterest enemies. At least, until the crisis of the Maurice debate in May 1918, Lloyd George's government seemed repeatedly on the brink of collapse, either from discord from within or from parliamentary assault from without. Almost miraculously Lloyd George was able to transcend every obstacle, to weather every crisis. More, he was able to transform the office of the premiership, even the substance of Cabinet government, in a way that was permanently to stamp its character on the British constitution. No premier has imposed more fundamental changes on the government and society of modern Britain.

From the start, his period at 10 Downing Street provoked acute controversy. In part, this was a result of his personal style. For the first time, as he himself wrote (not quite accurately) in his *War Memoirs*, there was a 'ranker' as prime minister, a man from the rank-and-file who had not passed through the training of a staff college or the older universities. He still felt himself to be very much the Welsh Baptist outsider; his associates were press lords or businessmen drawn from outside the usual political circles. His household at Downing Street was typically north Welsh in many ways – frugal and austere, as a result of Mrs Lloyd George's economical management. It was occasionally enlivened by the singing of Welsh hymns around the hearth. The prime minister went to bed early and rose early. By eight in the morning he had digested the news of the day and his official papers. He made a point of holding political conferences over breakfast, to the distress of Hankey and other advisers, who kept more conventional hours.

Lloyd George was also unusual in maintaining, in effect, an alternative household – Frances Stevenson's flat in central London where she had lived since 1915. Her relationship with

PREVIOUS PAGE Gas masks worn by soldiers of a machine gun unit at the front.

OPPOSITE Lloyd George relaxing at his Welsh home in Criccieth with his daughter Megan, September 1917.

Lloyd George with his much loved and respected 'Uncle Lloyd' whose death in 1917 as an old man of eighty-three helped to widen the gulf between Lloyd George and his Welsh ties.

the prime minister never overrode the claims of politics or of public duty, but clearly much care and some subterfuge had to be exercised to avoid a scandal. With her, Lloyd George found a calm release from the storms that beset his wartime premiership. Relations with Mrs Lloyd George, who still spent much time in Criccieth, naturally deteriorated, as they did with his eldest son Richard, and with his brother William. But the bonds that linked husband and wife survived all these unconventional strains, public and private – bonds perhaps of habit rather than love. Lloyd George's ties with Criccieth, and with his Welsh roots in general were becoming less firm. In February 1917, 'Uncle Lloyd', who had long been ailing, died at the age of eighty-three, to Lloyd George's deep distress. His death symbolised the snapping of some of the premier's abiding links with his native Wales. He was now more than ever a lonely figure, with a tense domestic life and with hangers-on rather than close friends. The fact that as prime minister he showed a remarkable gift to commune with the masses and that he established himself as one of the great mass leaders of the century only confirmed this position of lonely eminence.

But the controversy that surrounded the war premiership concerned his power far more than his style of life. No prime minister had ever exercised authority in so dictatorial a manner. Even in 1917 to 1918 were heard echoes of the charge, later developed by many critics in the inter-war period, that Lloyd George was ruling more in the manner of an American president, or perhaps a medieval monarch, with his own household advisers and private retainers. He was accused of turning Cabinet government into prime ministerial government, with power radiating uniquely from the lonely man at the centre.

From the start he transformed the instruments of central decision-making. He set up a new supreme War Cabinet of five men to run the war instead of the larger, more leisurely Cabinet of peacetime as maintained by Asquith. Bonar Law, the Unionist leader, was the only man to be given departmental responsibility, as Chancellor of the Exchequer; his major task, in fact, was the conciliation of parliament and Unionist critics at home while Lloyd George carried on with his efforts to win the war. Of the others, Curzon, another Unionist, and Arthur Henderson, leader of the Labour Party, were both given roving commissions as chairmen of Cabinet and *ad hoc* committees. Each was increasingly dominated by the imperious personality of the prime minister. Henderson was eventually to resign from the government in August 1917, while Curzon endured a thousand slights and rebuffs from Lloyd George (partly assuaged by the gift of a Marquisate) for almost six years. Most influential of all until the summer of 1918 was Lord Milner, a detached Imperialist removed from the usual party turmoil; with him Lloyd George's relations were very close. Milner's passion for broad executive power, his enthusiasm for empire, his interest in social reform, his contempt for ordinary party politics made him at first Lloyd George's most intimate ministerial colleague.

Over these men Lloyd George soon built up a personal ascendancy. It was even more marked over ministers not included in the charmed circle of the War Cabinet. Even ambitious subordinates like Winston Churchill (brought back into the government in July 1917 to strengthen its Liberal representation) complained in vain at their exclusion from the

Andrew Bonar Law, Unionist leader, who was appointed Chancellor of the Exchequer by Lloyd George; photograph by Bassano.

key decisions of strategy and policy generally. Most of the other new ministers were of little political importance. Many of them were not politicians at all – businessmen like Sir Joseph Maclay, Sir Eric Geddes and Lord Rhondda were a new breed of functional ministers brought in to do a job, with a limited brief to run their departments on brisk, businesslike lines without concerning themselves with the wider aspects of wartime policy.

More and more, it seemed that the Cabinet system was being dissolved. The War Cabinet was the shifting core of a broad range of hundreds of Cabinet committees and conferences of ministers, with military chiefs of staff and civil servants being brought in at will. Nothing more dramatically symbolised the change, and the way in which parliamentary control over the new system was being cut back, than the admission to the War Cabinet in June 1917 of General Jan Smuts of South Africa, who was not a British member of parliament at all. Smuts proved a valuable member of the government, but his presence confirmed how Lloyd George had built up his ascendancy over the Cabinet, parliament, the parties and the political world in general. The whole rambling new structure of wartime government, with a sprawling mass of committees branching outwards from it, all seemed to emphasise and magnify the power of the man at the centre. The contrast with Asquith's more leisured rule could not have been more marked.

This personal ascendancy of the prime minister was underpinned by other innovations. He created for the first time a Cabinet secretariat to arrange for the conduct of Cabinet business. Its secretary was a remarkable man, Sir Maurice Hankey, also the secretary of the Committee of Imperial Defence. He rapidly became a formidable influence on central government, on military policy and inter-allied diplomacy. At such key moments as the November 1917 conference at Rapallo, Hankey's role reinforced Lloyd George's command. His chief assistant was also a dominant personality in his way – the Welshman, Thomas Jones, an economist who was until recently a commissioner under the National Insurance Act. Jones and Hankey were never very close. Hankey, a conservative in his domestic views, distrusted Jones who had once been a Fabian socialist. Jones, he claimed, was 'a peacemonger and a syndicalist', with 'a sly Welsh face just like Lloyd George'. Still, their partnership was a formidable one until Lloyd George fell from power in October 1922. They made the Cabinet Office a forceful machine of government. They did far more than just arrange Cabinet agendas and record minutes, important

Sir Maurice Hankey, the formidable secretary of Lloyd George's Cabinet and previously of the Committee of Imperial Defence.

though these duties were. They were also in touch with all departments and all advisers, civilian and military, though responsible to the prime minister alone. They were, in Thomas Jones's rather chilling phrase, 'fluid persons moving amongst people who matter'. They extended their influence into major realms of policy-making, as parliamentary critics were quick to note in the post-war years. Hankey had much to do with post-war diplomacy, especially at Versailles; Jones was much involved with Ireland. Beyond them, the Cabinet secretariat included younger men like Leopold Amery, Mark Sykes and Lionel Curtis, all former protégés of Milner and members of his pre-war 'kindergarten' in South Africa. Historians have speculated whether Lloyd George swallowed up the kindergarten or was himself swallowed up by it. They pushed the government's policies in an imperialist and collectivist direction. In Philip Kerr they were to find an ideal agent for their views.

More symptomatic of the prime minister's new authority was another, more personal instrument – the prime minister's secretariat or 'Garden Suburb', so named because it met initially in huts in the garden of Number 10. It existed to carry out special inquiries on behalf of Lloyd George, and bring matters to his attention. It closely resembled the White House staff in the United States; Lloyd George was the first British premier to hire a 'brains trust' of 'the best and the brightest' to provide him with direct personal assistance. In practice, the division between the Cabinet Office and the 'Garden Suburb' was hard to determine, somewhat to Hankey's embarrassment. At first, the Garden Suburb consisted of only five members, all in their way characteristic advisers for Lloyd George. Waldorf Astor (owner of *The Observer* newspaper), and the Welsh industrialist, David Davies (soon to leave Lloyd George's service after a bitter quarrel) were both millionaires of cross-party views. Professor W.G.S. Adams was an All Souls professor of imperialist outlook. Joseph Davies was a Welsh businessman and commercial statistician who specialised in shipping: he was also used in 1917 in an attempted take-over of the anti-government *Westminster Gazette*, which showed the wide-ranging purposes to which the prime minister's private aides could be put. The most powerful member of the Garden Suburb was Philip Kerr, an austere, lonely man, a Christian Scientist, very much a disciple of Milner's 'social imperialism'. His special responsibility was foreign affairs. In particular he played a major part in the secret peace feelers put out to the Austrians in

Thomas Jones, the Welsh economist and chief assistant to Hankey. The latter distrusted this one-time Fabian socialist with 'a sly face just like Lloyd George'.

Lloyd George with Lord Milner, a member of the War Cabinet and Philip Kerr, the leading member of the Garden Suburb, who specialised in foreign affairs.

December 1917 and January 1918 when Lloyd George contemplated a possible settlement with the central powers to check the spread of Bolshevist socialism from Russia. From this time on, Kerr was a leading figure in Lloyd George's highly personal methods of summit diplomacy. Yet there were no constitutional checks upon his actions, from parliament, the Cabinet or anybody else apart from Lloyd George himself. Kerr's role showed dramatically how the wartime ascendancy had, at the level of decision-making, built up the prime minister's personal rule.

Beyond the Garden Suburb, there were other layers of

advisers. Close at hand there was Frances Stevenson as joint principal private secretary, along with J. T. Davies. There were other personal assistants, often Welshmen like John Rowlands, valuable trouble-shooters on the home front. There were also ambiguous men like Sir William Sutherland ('Bronco Bill'), a permissive go-between who acted as a link with the press. Sutherland, along with Kerr and others, was active in feeding government information to the press, in censoring information that came from opponents of the prime minister, and in conciliating press lords with favours or patronage. Since the newspapers to some extent took the place of parliament, during the party truce of wartime, in keeping political dialogue going at all, relations between the premier and the press were of crucial importance. Indeed, Lloyd George, mindful of the part played by the press in fostering his own career from the early 1880s to the crisis of December 1916, always gave this aspect of domestic politics his most careful attention. Sutherland's activities, backed up by the patronage exercised by Captain Freddie Guest, the government Liberal whip, and unofficial aid from press lords like Beaverbrook, showed that Lloyd George's personal rule had its ruthless side. But it was a desperate time. Perhaps without such methods as these the entire ministry would collapse, and with it the new ascendancy that Lloyd George had laboured to build up.

The crucial test of this new system of government was, of course, the running and winning of the war. Lloyd George's wartime premiership was punctuated by endless conflicts with naval and military authorities. His *War Memoirs* did more than justice to his own viewpoints, while Haig and others replied in kind. Both sides later on tended to exaggerate the extent of the wartime disagreements; still, there is no doubt that civilian–military relationships during the First World War were tense and embittered in a way quite unknown during Churchill's premiership of 1940 to 1945. The underlying cause of the conflict was that it was the first total war; no one was sure where the responsibility of the politicians ended and that of the generals and admirals began. Personal factors entered into it as well. Lloyd George deeply distrusted generals like Haig and Robertson, and military 'experts' generally. He deplored Haig's conventional approach to warfare, seen most clearly in Haig's failure to exploit the gains made by British tanks at the battle of Cambrai (November 1917). Haig had a blind faith, Lloyd George considered, in the role of the cavalry; their value, in Lloyd George's opinion, related more to gardening than to modern warfare. He preferred to rely on his own judgement and on congenial advisers like General Sir Henry Wilson, an Ulsterman. On their side, Haig and Robertson consorted freely with politicians like Asquith, with anti-government editors like J.A.Spender and A.G.Gardiner; they even tried to prejudice the King himself. No modern prime minister could now permit the politicial intrigue in which Haig and Robertson indulged in 1917 to 1918. It is not surprising that Lloyd George replied in kind, to impose civilian direction over war strategy. He was not averse to using the French, notably generals like Nivelle and Foch, to put pressure on the British commanders at the front; this was in large measure the point of his enthusiasm for 'unity of command' in France. To a degree, he succeeded.

With regard to the navy, Lloyd George managed to impose his will in 1917 without undue difficulty. In April 1917 the admirals and Sea Lords were compelled to accept his demands that they adopt the convoy system to ensure the safety of allied merchant shipping in the Atlantic. It may be guessed that Lloyd George's intention, announced on 25 April, to visit the Admiralty on the 30th and impose his will, helped to sway the naval chiefs to accept the convoy system two days later. The Admirals, wrote Lloyd George, had been persuaded 'not perhaps to take action, but to try action'. He then waged a steady campaign to remove the First Sea Lord, Admiral Jellicoe, whom he regarded as defeatist, particularly after the inconclusive battle at Jutland on 31 May 1916 had thrown doubt on the supremacy of the British Grand Fleet. Press support was used to put pressure on Jellicoe; even General Haig, alarmed at the submarine losses to British shipping, was used as an ally; private informers in the Admiralty like young commander Kenworthy gave Lloyd George additional material on the state of affairs in Admiralty House. By December 1917 Jellicoe had been removed: 'he will not be missed' was Lloyd George's grim comment. Carson, the First Lord of the Admiralty, who had for long defended Jellicoe, left the government shortly afterwards. With Lord Wemyss now established as First Sea Lord in place of Jellicoe, and Beatty as Commander of the Grand Fleet, civilian–naval relations were much more harmonious and Lloyd George had won a major triumph.

The generals were a far tougher obstacle, with Haig and Robertson well primed with political support. Lloyd George's reputation in military matters was highly questionable: it was not improved by his uncritical support of General Nivelle, a

Admiral Jellicoe, First Sea Lord, whom Lloyd George ousted from office in December 1917.

French Protestant commander who conducted a wholly disastrous offensive in May 1917. This was a costly failure, one which left the French army virtually incapable of waging a sustained offensive in western Europe for the remainder of the war. Mutinies testified to the collapse of French morale. In these circumstances, Lloyd George was unable to withstand the arguments of Haig in favour of a new British offensive in Flanders in the summer of 1917. One after another, the members of the War Cabinet, even finally Milner, came to accept Haig's dubious and often inaccurate proposals. Lloyd George, for once, was overruled by his own ministers, and had reluctantly to agree to an offensive in the Passchendaele region of Flanders in August. Any chance the scheme ever had was ruined by appalling weather. Haig ploughed stubbornly on: 324,000 British casualties were sacrificed in advancing just four miles. In three weeks over half a million British troops were lost,

Soldiers using duckboards to cross the appalling mud of the Passchendaele battleground, one of the most bloody and devastating offensives of the war, in which over half a million British troops died within three weeks.

many of them drowned in the mud. It was a murderous bloodbath: Siegfried Sassoon denounced it in a poem as 'a sepulchre of crime'. The British army was unable to resume the offensive for at least another nine months, and a defensive strategy was inevitable until assistance came from the United States. Lloyd George, more disillusioned than ever with the judgement of his military advisers, followed the dangerous practice of holding back reserves from the western front lest Haig should fritter them away a second time.

Lloyd George, however, was never one to despair. He now used political resource to undermine Haig and Robertson. The key was found at the conference at Rapallo in November 1917. Frances Stevenson noted in her diary (6 November): 'D. has made up his mind that General Robertson has got to have his power taken away from him.' With Hankey's aid, a plan was drawn up to create a new Supreme Allied War Council at Versailles, an implied rival to Robertson's Imperial General Staff. In February 1918 Robertson was offered the dilemma of staying where he was, or of moving to the unknown hazards of the new War Council. Either way, he would lose his authority. Lloyd George was never closer to falling from power. He told Philip Kerr that they might be packing their bags in a week. Opposition politicians, from Asquith downwards backed Robertson up. So did some Liberal journals (which Lloyd George later scathingly dismissed as 'cocoa slop'). He narrowly survived a parliamentary attack on 19 February, in which he triumphed despite suffering from one of those heavy colds to

which he was prone at times of nervous stress. But, at terrible cost to his own physical resources, survive he did. It was Robertson who fell. Neither Haig nor Derby, the War Minister, would back him up in the ultimate crisis: not for nothing was it said of Derby that 'like a feather pillow he bears the imprint of the person who last sat on him'. Robertson was 'kicked upstairs' and was succeeded as CIGS by General Sir Henry Wilson, a more earthy and congenial figure than the truculent 'Wully' Robertson. Thereafter, the so-called 'X Committee' of the War Cabinet, consisting of Milner, Wilson and Lloyd George, asserted its control of war policy. Civilian, and therefore prime ministerial, authority over military affairs had been partially vindicated. Lloyd George's new ascendancy had been confirmed. His control of governmental power was more complete.

Over decision-making generally, Lloyd George's authority became more and more pronounced. As Arthur Henderson later observed, 'L.G. was the War Cabinet and no one else counted.' With the assistance of Kerr and other aides, he was largely in charge of wartime diplomacy. It was he who took command of conferences; he who tried to stiffen the resolve of the Italians after a disastrous defeat at Caporetto (November 1917); he who promoted the peace feelers of the winter of 1917 to 1918; he who laboured for 'unity of command' with the French; he who tried to speed up American support for the Allies in early 1918. Balfour, the Foreign Secretary, had a subordinate role; his policy was 'a free hand for the little man'.

Lord Derby, Minister for War, and Lloyd George in the garden of 10 Downing Street.

At the same time, Lloyd George had the energy to turn his attention to the home front also. He took a particular interest in labour relations, a key factor in the production of munitions and newly inflamed after the triumph of the Bolshevik revolution in Russia in October 1917. Lloyd George strove hard to persuade labour that the government was bent on social reform – a point he drove home in wartime visits to factories. He upheld collective bargaining, the rise in basic wage rates, and improved working conditions that the war had brought with it. In a notable address to the trade unions at Westminster Hall on 5 January 1918 he strove successfully to counteract the damaging effects of the news of the secret treaties, now released by the new Russian government. He argued that the government aimed at a post-war world free from the old slavery of empire and class rule, a world which would safeguard economic collaboration and national self-determination for all peoples. The publication of President Woodrow Wilson's 'Fourteen Points' shortly afterwards reinforced Lloyd George's appeal to labour and radical opinion. His careful attention to labour relations, without precedent by any previous prime minister, and partly a legacy of his knowledge of the labour world since his days at the Board of Trade in 1905 to 1908, produced results. The domestic scene was comparatively peaceful for the remainder of the war. There were those who wanted to go further and who meditated forming a 'patriotic labour' movement to counteract the 'Bolshevists and pacifists' said to be dominant in the Labour Party. Milner advocated this idea, but it proved to be a complete illusion.

Lloyd George's direct personal authority was best shown, perhaps, by his interventions in the dreary problems of Ireland. Even with all his other exhausting commitments at home and abroad, he still found time to intervene to direct the course of policy towards Ireland. All the major decisions about Ireland in 1917 and 1918 were made, not by the Chief Secretary for Ireland as had invariably been the case down to 1916, but by the prime minister. It was he who set up the abortive conference in May 1917 which tried in vain to produce a last minute compromise over Home Rule. It was he who reacted to the failure of the convention in April 1918 with a desperate attempt to link Home Rule with the imposing of military conscription on the Irish. He also enforced martial law throughout southern Ireland. The results were disastrous. Irish nationalist opinion, already passionately inflamed by the execution of Sir Roger Casement and the leaders of the 1916 Easter rising in Dublin, now flocked to support Sinn Fein, who preached Republicanism. Relations between Great Britain and Catholic southern Ireland deteriorated alarmingly, while Lloyd George himself appeared seriously to underestimate the strength of Sinn Fein influence in the south. The 'troubles' of 1918, the prolonged violence in southern Ireland, destined to scar Anglo-Irish relations for over half a century, were already in the making. In his Irish failures, as much as in his other achievements, the roots of Lloyd George's dominance as a wartime leader must be discerned.

As the supreme decision-maker, in charge of key policies from the trenches in France to the Irish countryside, his authority became steadily more emphatic. It was an authority, however, that rested on his control at the centre of government. In the wider political arena, on the periphery, his standing was far more uncertain. At each level of political support, Lloyd George, so dominant elsewhere, was the most precarious of premiers. His downfall seemed imminent from week to week. Only extraordinary feats of political equilibrism appeared to keep his ministry in being.

He had, for instance, only a limited command over parliament. His majority there was always uncertain: Asquith sat on the front Opposition bench as a permanent alternative prime minister. The allegiance of dozens of Liberals was uncertain, with the authority over them of the government whips almost negligible. Unionist backbench support was also hard to determine, for all the loyalty shown to his leader by Bonar Law. In a supreme crisis like the Robertson affair in February 1918 Lloyd George could only guess intuitively whether he could continue in office, especially as the war continued to go badly until the summer of 1918. Admittedly the ministry had been strengthened in parliament in July 1917 by the co-opting of two first-class Liberal debaters: Edwin Montagu, formerly a close associate of Asquith who had married his young girl-friend, Venetia Stanley, and Winston Churchill, who had been in the shadows since the Dardanelles failure. These appointments helped to counteract the swelling army of disappointed critics on the backbenches.

Sir Frederick Maurice, who denounced Lloyd George for his mishandling of the war in early 1918 and produced statistics to back his accusations.

Even so, the government faced an acute crisis in the House as late as May 1918. Once again its fall seemed imminent. The crisis arose as a result of charges made in the press by General Sir Frederick Maurice, until April the head of Military Intelligence. He now claimed that Lloyd George and Bonar Law had lied to the House about the extension of the British fighting line in France at the start of 1918. Implicit in his charges was the belief that Lloyd George had deliberately starved Haig of reinforcements in the six months since Passchendaele. The prime minister was accused of responsibility for the holocaust of casualties suffered by the British army on the western front. He decided to meet the charge head-on, with a fierce counter-attack in parliament. Assuming almost single-handed the defence of the government's military record, he produced figures to uphold his claim that British military strength was greater at the start of 1918 than a year earlier. Most effective of all, he claimed that his figures were supplied by Maurice's own department. Maurice was as guilty as anyone if Haig had been deliberately starved of reinforcements. Lloyd George's facts and figures have provoked much debate: it now looks as if Maurice was probably right, but it remains unclear whether

Lloyd George realised that his statistics were incorrect. Frances Stevenson has a story of a draft of the correct figures being found subsequently by her and one of the prime minister's private secretaries, J.T.Davies, and of the documents being deliberately burnt. But which draft was it? The truth of the matter remains shrouded in mystery. What is indisputable is that Lloyd George's counter-attack was entirely triumphant. Henceforth, the government was able to face with confidence all threats to its parliamentary position. A notable by-product of the debate was a deepening chasm between pro- and anti-government Liberals. Those one hundred and six members who voted against the government in the Maurice debate included ninety-eight Liberals. From now on, most of them would be marked down as declared opponents – not unreasonably in view of their record, and in view of the fact that the Maurice vote was virtually one of confidence in the government. The Maurice debate, for all its complexities, played a major role in the division of the Liberal Party and its post-war enfeeblement. In the short run, it ensured that Lloyd George had for the first time a permanent measure of control over the House of Commons.

Elsewhere Lloyd George's power was still more questionable. One aspect of this which worried him was the press from which so many of the criticisms launched at his government had derived. As has been seen, Sutherland and others were active in ensuring a flow of information and news favourable to the government. Censorship, and even the invention of news, were widely practised; tales of German atrocities, of 'the brutal butchers of Berlin', circulated freely. In addition, Lloyd George spent much time and trouble in winning over newspaper editors and proprietors. He consorted with press lords like Riddell, Rothermere and Beaverbrook, and offered them posts in the government if necessary. He had a lengthy flirtation with Lord Northcliffe, the owner of *The Times*. Northcliffe seemed to have built up a position of political importance after a mission to the United States in the late summer of 1917. But on his return in November he clashed fatally with Lloyd George over an offer of the Air Ministry. He grossly flouted the rules by revealing the offer and using this to make a public attack on the government's conduct of the war. Despite a temporary reconciliation when Northcliffe ran enemy propaganda, Lloyd George and Northcliffe later became implacable enemies, while the press lord's dreams of himself as a man of destiny, proved empty and pathetic. Lloyd George could do

Lloyd George with Lord Riddell, the newspaper proprietor, in 1917.

nothing to prevent *The Times*'s relentless hostility towards himself for the remainder of his premiership. But when an opportunity came to buy out an opposition journal, he acted swiftly and unforgivingly. In October 1918 a *coup* was staged which saw a businessmen's syndicate, headed by the pro-government Liberal member Sir Henry Dalziel (with whom Lloyd George had toured Argentina back in 1896) buy up the *Daily Chronicle*. Its editor, Robert Donald, formerly one of Lloyd George's golfing companions at Walton Heath, had been playing with fire: he had even hired General Maurice as his newspaper's military correspondent. In two days (3 to 5 October 1918) Donald was told that the prime minister had resented his recent attacks, that almost two million pounds had been privately put up, and that his editorship had come to an end. Henceforth the *Daily Chronicle* was closely associated with the Lloyd Georgian brand of Liberalism. A major vehicle of radical criticism was silenced. Even so, Lloyd George's control over the

Alfred Harmsworth, Lord Northcliffe, as a young man. He and Lloyd George became implacable enemies and *The Times* remained constantly hostile to Lloyd George's actions.

press remained a source of anxiety throughout the wartime years. The fourth estate could not be dominated as easily as the third.

Over the wider political public, Lloyd George's authority was more debatable. More than any previous prime minister he tried to establish a direct relationship with the public. His visits to factories and servicemen at the front were widely publicised. His attendance at the national *eisteddfod* in August of each year was a major spectacle. At Aberystwyth he charmed his audience by urging 'let the people sing' and comparing the music of the Welsh people to the nightingale that sang at the darkest hour of the night. His dominating presence, his flowing white mane and his Tyrolean cloak were immediately recognised, as newsreels of the time confirm. Even so, his hold on public opinion was most uncertain. In Ireland, he was becoming a detested figure, as was virtually every other British statesman. In the world of labour, rank-and-file militants

Lloyd George talking to British soldiers at the front. Despite his widely publicised and well-attended public appearances, by 1918 Lloyd George's popularity with the general public was insecure.

rejected the government's call for consensus. Local soviets were formed in mining areas, notably in South Wales, while there were fears of social revolution in Glasgow and Clydeside. The Labour Party, fragmented and dispirited for much of the earlier part of the war, substantially increased its following and moved confidently to the left. Clearly Lloyd George's wider standing as a wartime leader, beyond the narrow world of decision-making at Westminster and Whitehall, was fragile indeed. What, many wondered, would happen to Lloyd George's ascendancy once the normal world of peacetime politics, dominated by party alignments, was restored?

To try to create a political future for himself, he had somehow to give himself a party base. After all, a prime minister without a party was liable to sink without trace at any moment. He was still a Liberal member of parliament, and many Liberals supported his government. But Asquith remained the party leader, while the party organisation was overwhelmingly loyal to him, save only in Wales. The events of December 1916 were felt by many Liberals to have produced an unbridgeable gulf between Liberals who supported Asquith and those favourable to the prime minister. There were casual talks during 1917 to consider the formation of some kind of 'Lloyd George party'. Dr Christopher Addison, a Liberal medical doctor who had played a part in rallying Liberal support behind Lloyd George in December 1916, was active in these discussions as was Waldorf Astor of *The Observer*. It was rumoured that Lord Beaverbrook was being approached to try to finance a new pro-government party. Captain Guest, the worldly Liberal whip, began negotiations with pro-government sympathisers in the business and press worlds to try to amass a party fund to support candidates. But it all seemed fruitless. Indeed, Lloyd George himself remembered well the fate of Joseph Chamberlain and was reluctant to sever permanently his relations with the orthodox Liberal machine in which he had spent his career. Until the late spring of 1918, then, Lloyd George's political future seemed completely obscure. It seemed probable that his wartime premiership would prove to be a brilliant but temporary interlude.

After the Maurice debate in May 1918 the first tentative steps were taken to set up a pro-Lloyd George party of 'Coalition Liberals'. Addison and Guest were the main agents in this move. The new organisation had neither a fixed membership nor a positive programme. It existed simply to perpetuate the political future of Lloyd George: it was just a personal connection like those that flourished in the eighteenth century. But it was at least a start, and provided some kind of blueprint for what the premier's post-war role might be.

That summer, the need to ensure Lloyd George's future, to establish some kind of continuity between wartime and post-war politics became imperative. In July 1918 the first moves were begun to concoct an electoral arrangement between the pro-government Liberals, represented by Captain Guest, and Bonar Law's Unionist Party. A preliminary list of pro-government Liberal candidates was drawn up, with possible constituencies marked out for them in which they would be free from Unionist opposition at the next election. Lloyd George himself took a close interest in these discussions, as well he might. It was apparently he who demanded that the number of pro-government Liberal candidates be guaranteed to be as many as one hundred and fifty, and who ensured, therefore, a substantial share of the spoils for the weaker members of the Coalition. This was the origin of the famous or notorious 'coupon' given to candidates sympathetic to the government, a factor which did perhaps more than anything else to stir up internecine discord amongst the Liberals after the war. Without doubt, it made the gulf between Lloyd George and Asquith, then still bridgeable, all the more bitter and more permanent.

The 'coupon' was conceived in terms of a wartime election being held. Lloyd George himself seems to have assumed gloomily that war would drag on through 1919, perhaps until the summer of 1920, when the military and economic might of the United States would make itself felt. Then in August and September 1918 the military situation dramatically changed on the western front. Until then virtual stalemate had continued: indeed, it was the Germans who had come nearest to effecting a breakthrough, since their spring offensive in north-east France in April had been contained by only the most desperately narrow margin. In fact, the offensive proved to be the Germans' last throw: it exhausted German resources and morale. In addition, at long last American forces came over in such numbers that they substantially reinforced allied strength in France. In August Haig finally forced a breakthrough and an allied advance began towards the German frontier. For the next few weeks the German armies were visibly in retreat. Austria–Hungary meanwhile was withdrawing from effective participation in the war, while in Palestine and Syria the Turks were being pushed back by Allenby's British and imperial troops. Most dramatic of all, Germany itself suddenly under-

The Brandenburg Gate under fire from royalist troops following the Berlin revolution of November 1918.

went internal disintegration. War weariness, the impact of soldiers' and workers' soviets in several German cities, the long-term effects on food supplies of the allied naval blockade caused the German government to collapse. At the end of October the Hapsburg empire broke up in Austria–Hungary. The Hohenzollern régime in Germany was on the point of suffering the same fate. The historic dynasties of central Europe were dissolving. Lloyd George's political future was therefore a matter for urgent and immediate decision.

In September and October 1918 he was largely engaged in seizing the initiative to try to create a post-war settlement. (He was also a temporary victim of the virulent influenza epidemic that struck Europe at this time.) He took the fateful decision to retain allied forces in Russia, at least for the moment. He was locked in fierce conflict with the French government of Clemenceau over the precise details of the parcelling out of French and British claims in the Near East in Palestine, Syria and the Arab lands. The presence of immense oil deposits in this region lent urgency to the dispute. He protested vigorously against aspects of Woodrow Wilson's 'Fourteen Points' as they affected British national interests; in particular he criticised the demand for 'freedom of the seas' which would frustrate Britain's traditional claim to the right of search of neutral shipping. Above all, after having previously been an advocate of a moderate post-war settlement, he now argued vigorously in the Cabinet for stern treatment of Germany, for the trial of the Kaiser and other leaders, for heavy reparation claims from Germany to pay for war damage, and for the possible occupation of the west bank of the Rhineland. He and Clemenceau, whatever their other differences, were agreed on full compensation being paid by the Germans to the allied nations for losses caused by the German forces on land, sea and in the air. War guilt would be riveted on Germany alone. In all these issues, it was Lloyd George who was now assuming the initiative, taking a strongly nationalist line, apparently striving to establish the same overwhelming dominance in the international scene that he had done at home.

But domestic politics were never far from his thoughts, expecially as the war drew to a seemingly inevitable close in November 1918. Indeed, the connection between internal and international politics – for instance, in relation to the spread of Bolshevism – was always present in his mind. In November the 'coupon' agreement with Bonar Law of the previous July was now made into an unshakable alliance. A hundred and fifty seats were set aside, as arranged, for the pro-government Liberals. In addition, Lloyd George managed to ensure that the government's manifesto at the ensuing general election would have a marked Liberal flavour and would be one that Liberals could honourably support. With qualifications in every case, Irish Home Rule, free trade, social reconstruction, even old issues like House of Lords' reform and Welsh disestablishment, all formed part of the new government's intended programme. Lloyd George clearly saw himself as far more than just a Unionist puppet. Indeed, at times his old enthusiasm for social reform was re-charged by the prospect of a new political era, freed from the old incubus of party politics. He even hoped that the Labour Party might join his post-war coalition after the election. But, not surprisingly, the vast majority of Labour delegates at a specially convened conference declared outright opposition to participating in a post-war capitalist government. The dramatist, Bernard Shaw, successfully urged the conference: 'Go back to Lloyd George and say – "Nothing doing"!'

Even so, a sufficient number of 'patriotic' Labour leaders, including such respected figures as George Barnes, lined up behind the government to lend plausibility to Lloyd George's claim that his government had all-party support. Its Liberal backing was much stronger. The Coalition Liberal ministers now included not only controversial figures like Churchill and Addison, but also a dignified intellectual like the Oxford historian, H.A.L. Fisher. The editor of the *Manchester Guardian*, C.P. Scott, the keeper of the tablets of Gladstonian orthodoxy, retained his faith in the prime minister's Liberal credentials. When the coalition's manifesto was presented to a meeting of Liberal members in the House on 12 November 1918, the day after the armistice, it was carried with acclamation. An approach was even made to possible opponents. Asquith was offered the Lord Chancellorship, with the promise of being able to nominate two of the government's secretaryships of state. There is no evidence to suggest that this offer by Lloyd George was insincere. He was far from wanting Tory bedfellows alone in his new government: the career of Joseph Chamberlain, the

BELOW LEFT C. P. Scott, editor of the *Manchester Guardian* and staunch Liberal supporter of Lloyd George.

BELOW RIGHT H. A. L. Fisher, the Oxford historian and leading Liberal, who joined Lloyd George's Coalition ministry.

lapsed hero of British radicalism, was grave warning against such an approach. Lloyd George wanted to be a truly national leader, heading a government in which pre-war Liberal principles would have their honoured place. Only such a government, Lloyd George claimed, could steer a middle course of sanity between Bolshevist revolutionaries and Tory diehards. The wild men on both sides could be sloughed off. The failure of Asquith to respond to these overtures, and the decision of his allies like Simon, McKenna and Runciman to declare relentless hostility to the new coalition after the war, played their part in the later decline of the Liberal Party. Responsibility was far from being Lloyd George's alone, though undoubtedly he had his share.

At the general election campaign in late November and early December, Lloyd George dominated the political stage. More than any previous prime minister, more than Chatham, the younger Pitt or Palmerston, he dictated the framework of political debate. His speeches were the highlights of the campaign and drew immense crowds everywhere. The campaign, wrote a Welsh journal, was a 'ceremony of congratulation' to 'the man who won the war'. Lloyd George's campaign speeches were in the main low-keyed. Despite his belligerent line in private about post-war treatment of Germany, his public addresses at first were moderate in their attitude. He made a real attempt, quite contrary to what was argued by Keynes and other critics later on, to educate the public in the need for conciliation and for the recognition of the fact that all nations, victors and vanquished, had to live peaceably together, free from vengeance. He cited the 'reconstruction' of the southern states after the American civil war (Lloyd George could always draw on an extensive fund of historical analogy) as an example of imposed retribution by the victors leading to enduring bitterness. It was lesser members of the government who produced much of the jingoism at this election – notably Sir Eric Geddes who urged an enthusiastic crowd at Cambridge that Germany should 'be squeezed until the pips squeaked'. Asquithian and Labour speakers were almost as belligerent in their references to Germany. But Lloyd George's later speeches did show a tendency to be carried along by the floodtide of jingoism. In particular, he delivered an unlucky off-the-cuff statement at Bristol on 11 December – one which he later regretted – in which he demanded that Germany should pay the uttermost cost of the war. He also suggested that a more optimistic construction could be placed on Germany's capacity

Lloyd George addressing a Welsh crowd at Lampeter Station, Cardiganshire, just after the end of the war.

to pay than was suggested by the financial experts. In addition, it was undeniable that the pro-government newspapers, and many 'couponed' candidates, Unionist, Liberal and Labour, lent their voices to nationalist hysteria of the most irresponsible kind. Many wondered whether Lloyd George could ever control the terrifying 'patriotic' juggernaut on which he was to ride into the post-war world.

Inevitably, the government won a huge majority at the polls. Lloyd George finished up with over five hundred and twenty supporters, of whom one hundred and thirty-six were Coalition

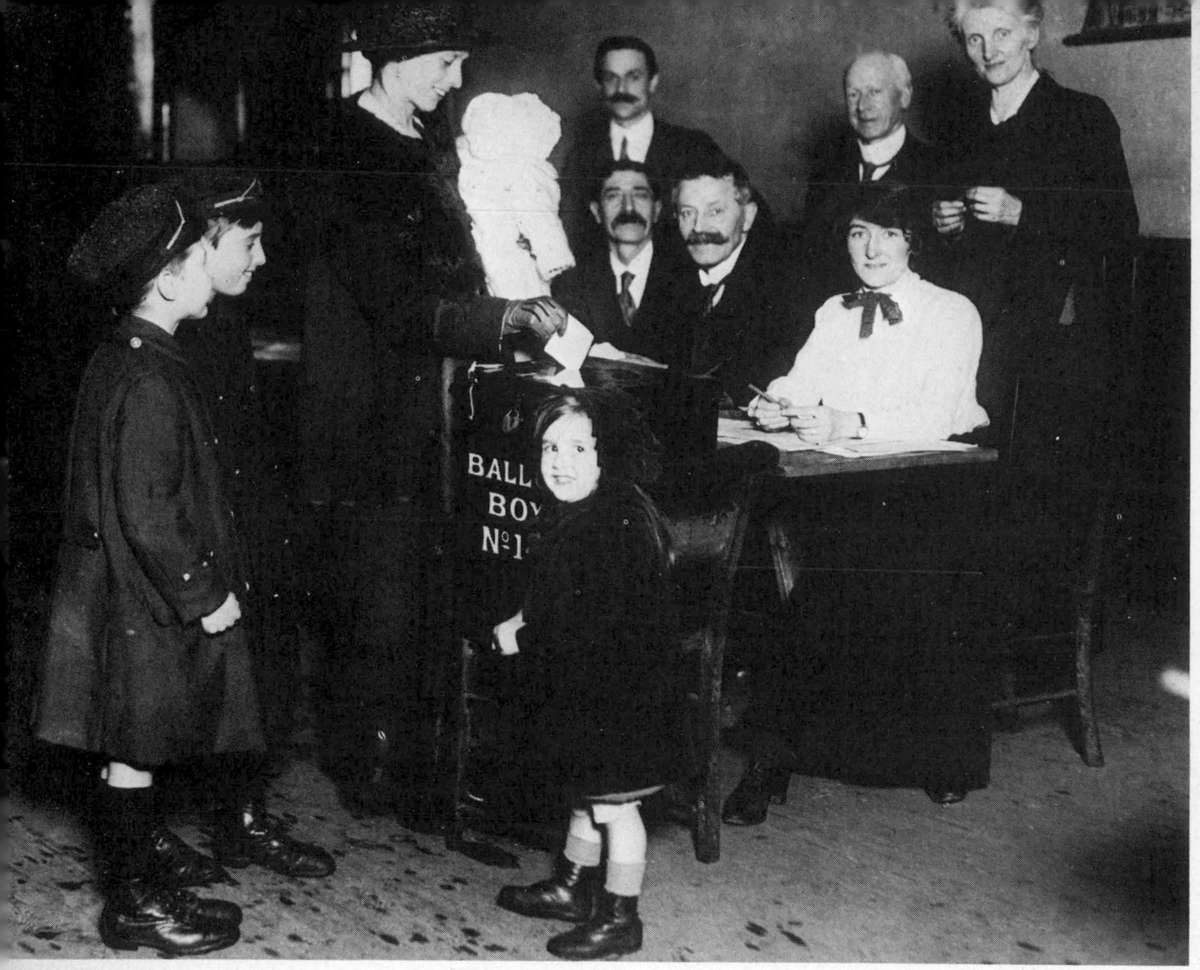

A woman voting at Lloyd George's 'coupon election' of December 1918 – the first election in which women were able to vote.

Liberals and most of the rest Unionist. The opposition (excluding the Irish Sinn Feiners who refused to take their seats at Westminster) numbered a mere fifty-seven Labour and only about twenty-five Asquithian 'Independent Liberals' (derisively dubbed the 'Wee Frees'). The government's triumph was complete; Lloyd George himself was indubitably the architect of it. Bonar Law wrote at this time, 'He can be Prime Minister for life if he likes.' Lloyd George himself was less certain. He had, after all, seen a 'khaki election' before in 1900, and well knew how patriotic euphoria could dissolve almost overnight. The false unity of the 'coupon election' could soon enough give way to the usual party and class divisions. Even so, the election was a remarkable popular endorsement of the supra-party, almost supra-political, position which he had attained since December 1916. For a moment, on the threshold of a world again at peace, he seemed to be the unique arbiter of Britain's destinies. The premiership, perhaps British politics as a whole, might never be the same again.

No one has ever disputed that Lloyd George's wartime

premiership brought with it unprecedented changes in British politics and society. What is more debatable is how lasting these transformations were. In some ways, he remodelled the premiership in a way that was to leave a permanent stamp on the constitution. The Cabinet secretariat, more powerful instruments of government at the centre, would be permanent features of every premiership henceforth. The state was to intervene in people's lives as never before. But whether more personal instruments such as the Garden Suburb, and the highly individual roles of advisers like Philip Kerr would survive in the post-war era was harder to predict. The usual restraints on the presidential style of leadership would be more powerful in a world freed from the scourge of total war. The British never liked dictators: one Cromwell was enough. Britain had no Bonapartist tradition and would never need one.

Again, the effect of Lloyd George's wartime premiership on party politics was unclear. Many sensed, despite the unnatural landslide produced by the 'coupon election', that the Labour Party would soon build up its strength amongst a newly enlarged and largely working-class electorate. Nor was the Liberal Party necessarily the divided and shattered rump that the polls seemed to suggest; reunion was not out of the question. And how long the Unionists under Bonar Law would remain happy to cling to Lloyd George's coat-tails was even harder to determine. What could be said was that the issues, even the language of politics, had been radically changed. Lloyd George's premiership had coincided with the virtual disappearance of the old church-and-chapel politics of his youth. Welsh disestablishment was a time-worn distraction of interest only to the bishops and individualists like Lord Robert Cecil. Free Trade was no longer the hallowed Liberal shibboleth it had been before 1914: Lloyd George's administration had continued measures begun under Asquith in 1915 to 1916 to protect 'key' domestic industries, to prevent foreign dumping of cheap imports and to give preference to colonial products. Lords' reform and temperance were equally casualties of the war, and Lloyd George's running of it. Instead, politics were now dominated by the beguiling word 'reconstruction': which could mean anything from left-wing social reforms to right-wing economic nationalism and attacks on alien immigrants. In all these ways, Edwardian Britain, and its political divisions, seemed decades away. In so far as Lloyd George was still a fresh and uncommitted figure, one who could make the transition from pre-war party conflicts to the new themes of post-1918, his prospects were rosy. Indeed, for the moment any political alignment that did not include Lloyd George at its centre, simply did not make sense. As 'the man who won the war' he was, for the present, the indispensable leader.

Whether he was to remain in office, however, depended ultimately on what the mood of British society really was. In many ways, Britain had been turned into a more progressive and egalitarian country during the war. Working men, women, the younger generation, had all gained from a new mood of equality and social opportunity. Education, housing, working conditions, had been substantially reformed. There seemed a widespread mood of impatience with pre-war conventions, as there was to be again in 1945. But it remained to be seen how this new climate would fit in with Lloyd George's concept of national unity. The post-war society might produce more acute party conflict, more intense social divisions. Lloyd George's system of streamlined presidential government, exploiting the theme of 'one nation', might not so easily adapt to a more democratic age, increasingly dominated by the clash between capital and organised labour. It might be harder now to sustain the view that Lloyd George was truly leader of all the people, not merely its top echelons, that he was both radical and responsible, left-wing and moderate, at the same time. Could it even turn out that Lloyd George, the greatest innovator ever to assume the premiership, the most total outsider ever to take over the supreme command, might finish up in his turn as a dated figure, ill-suited for the politics of post-war? To most working men at least, his claim to be the special champion of the under-dog had been severely dented by the 'coupon election'. He had now become the ally of anti-socialist red-baiters of the crudest kind, an exponent of the 'red scare' technique. By contrast, to Unionist diehards he was still the 'big beast', a dangerous animal who swept conventions aside and treated all institutions with contempt. Even at the moment of his greatest triumph in December 1918, he seemed as many-sided and enigmatic as ever. For him, most of the options were still open. His destiny was still in the melting pot. Would he build a new 'national politics' upon the consensus of the wartime years, harnessing the new mood of dynamic change? Or would it be Lloyd George, rather than apparently discredited failures like the Labour leader, Ramsay MacDonald, who would prove to be the supreme casualty of the First World War?

5

LEADER IN PEACE
1919-22

After the triumphant outcome of the 'coupon election' Lloyd George appeared to occupy a position of unchallengeable dominance in British politics. There were few obstacles to a smooth transition from the emergency leadership of wartime to a new style of peacetime presidential government. At first, the conventions of the war years were retained. The War Cabinet and the Garden Suburb were retained; parliament was muffled; public attention was dazzlingly focused on the bewildering activities of 'the man who won the war'. Ministers who stepped out of line were ruthlessly slapped down. Even Churchill, now Secretary of State for War, was harshly reminded in January 1919 of his duty to observe his prime minister's orders when he followed an individual line over demobilisation of the armed forces. A former close associate like Milner was cast aside when he showed signs of declining powers. The prime minister launched accusations against him of 'dilatoriness and neglect' in full Cabinet. By the end of 1919 there were widespread charges that Lloyd George was turning himself into something near a dictator. These charges were not allayed by the reluctant restoration of the full Cabinet by the prime minister in October 1919. For the Cabinet seemed now almost to be turning into an irrelevance. It was being bypassed by secret committees and 'conferences of ministers', totally dependent on the whim of the prime minister and his faithful Garden Suburb. By early 1920 many writers in the press were commenting on the manner in which Lloyd George neglected or browbeat colleagues. They deplored the discordant notes of the one-man band.

Many of these charges were exaggerated. As the head of the Cabinet, Lloyd George was tolerant and sympathetic. In 1920, as always, he was the best and most receptive of listeners, at his most effective when presiding over and summing up complex arguments in Cabinet. Again, many of the fears voiced about the roles of the Garden Suburb and the Cabinet Office, and their interventions in policy-making, were far-fetched. Even so, there is no doubt that the premiership underwent a qualitative change in the immediate post-war years. Lloyd George commanded the executive machine in a manner true of none of his predecessors, least of all of Asquith. In the press and in the parliamentary lobbies, journalists and backbenchers voiced fears that Lloyd George was undermining Cabinet government, collective responsibility, the liberties of parliament, even the very balance of the constitution itself. Men quoted Dunning's resolution, directed against George III's government in 1780,

PREVIOUS PAGE The allied leaders at 10 Downing Street in 1918; (left to right) Foch and Clemenceau (of France), Lloyd George, Orlando and Sonnino (of Italy).

to the effect that Lloyd George's power had increased, was increasing, and ought to be diminished. These fears provided the background against which the pattern of post-war politics unfolded.

The nature of his peacetime premiership was initially determined by his role at the peace negotiations in Paris between January and July 1919. While Bonar Law held the fort at home and the Cabinet kept government ticking over in the domestic sphere until the premier returned home, Lloyd George, along with Clemenceau, the French prime minister, and President Woodrow Wilson of the United States, was one of the major architects of the peace settlement. Many legends have accumulated around his conduct of the negotiations in Paris. It was alleged that he was unusually devious and deceitful; in contrast, for instance, with the uncompromising nobility displayed by

The major architects of the Paris peace settlement – the French prime minister Clemenceau, the US President Woodrow Wilson and Lloyd George – at Versailles, after signing the Peace Treaty in 1919.

Woodrow Wilson. In fact, as Harold Nicolson pointed out, Lloyd George combined flexibility of method with rare consistency of aim. Perhaps alone of the three major peacemakers he had long-term objectives in Europe, for which he worked with patience and resource. He was also accused, notably by J. M. Keynes in *The Economic Consequences of the Peace*, of pursuing a vindictive policy of crushing Germany by punitive reparations in line with the 'jingo' atmosphere of the 'coupon election' of 1918. In fact, Lloyd George was the most persistent advocate of moderation throughout the entire conference. In the final Council of Four meetings in June and July 1919 he strove hard, though with limited success, to revise the peace terms to be offered to Germany. In some areas, certainly, he took a narrow view of British interests, as did all the British delegation. He was anxious to retain British mandated territories in the Near East, with their valuable oil supplies. He strove to maintain Britain's right of search of naval vessels on the high seas in the face of the American demand for the 'freedom of the seas'. He upheld Britain's claims to the German colonies in Africa, notably Tanganyika. Nevertheless, in Paris he showed himself capable of taking a broader view. There, as so often in domestic politics, he was above all the conciliator, anxious to restore peace and prosperity to a shattered continent. If the Versailles settlement in later years was to help in generating nationalist grievances in Germany (aided, in part, by exaggerated claims by Keynes that Germany had been economically crushed almost beyond redemption) Lloyd George was the least guilty of the peacemakers. Amidst the babel of pressures and recriminations, the vindictive campaigns of papers like *The Times*, right-wing protests in the British parliament, the erratic behaviour of Woodrow Wilson in pursuit allegedly of 'peace without victory', it was Lloyd George who pursued the steadiest course.

From the start of the conference, he was an advocate of leniency. He tried to scale down the reparation payments to be imposed on Germany. He argued forcibly that the more statesmanlike course would be to try to build up the economies of the new nations of central and eastern Europe, victors and vanquished alike, so that trade and economic intercourse could be restored. He criticised the exaggerated claims of the money to be obtained from Germany made by the French Finance Minister, Klotz, 'the only Jew who knows nothing about money' as he was sardonically called. Equally, Lloyd George demanded a moderate policy in relation to Germany's new frontiers. He fought to have the large German-speaking populations of Danzig, Upper Silesia and the Rhineland kept under German control. As a Welshman he had some special understanding of national minorities. He argued that to transfer populations to alien control would both breed nationalist resentment in Germany and also perhaps make it a prey to Bolshevist subversion from Soviet Russia. At the same time, he was anxious not to make the new Russian régime an international outcast either. Both Germany and Russia, he argued, should be represented in the new League of Nations, while trade relations with eastern Europe should be restored as soon as possible, on political and economic grounds.

In March 1919 he drafted a notable memorandum in a castle in the forest of Fontainebleau, outside Paris. This document, prepared by Lloyd George, Hankey, Smuts and General

Lloyd George, with Esmond Harmsworth and J. T. Davies, two of his private secretaries, arriving at Fontainebleau. Frances Stevenson, who accompanied Lloyd George throughout, is on the right.

Sir Henry Wilson, and written up by the ever-present Philip Kerr, was an eloquent demand for moderation; perhaps the first positive blow struck for appeasement in the post-war period. It was a despairing protest at the path which the peace conference had so far followed – the path of vengeance.

> When nations are exhausted by wars in which they have put forth all their strength, and which leave them tired, bleeding and broken, it is not difficult to patch up a peace that may last until the generation which experienced the war has passed away. . . . What is difficult is to draw up a peace which will not provoke a fresh struggle when those who have had practical experience of what war means have passed away.

Germany, the memorandum stated, would always be a first-class power, and this should be openly recognised. Reparation payments should be scaled down drastically according to Germany's capacity to pay. German-speaking populations should not be forcibly placed under French or Polish rule. While the Kaiser and other wartime leaders should be brought to trial, the German people should not be made international scapegoats. But the effect of all this on the ultimate peace terms imposed on the reluctant German delegation in July was limited. There were a few concessions like making Danzig a free city and the plebiscite in Upper Silesia (achieved in spite of Wilson's opposition), but not much more. In the face of Wilson's moralistic bitterness towards the German aggressors, and Clemenceau's grim resolve that France should never again be invaded as in August 1914, Lloyd George made limited headway. There was a major departure in April while he was away for a few days in London addressing the House of Commons and heading off a right-wing revolt. In his absence, the French managed to slip through an allied decision to occupy the west bank of the Rhineland (on a non-separatist basis) for the next fifteen years.

Even so, Lloyd George gained enough of his objectives at Paris to produce at least a defensible settlement. Liberals and radicals hailed it, on his return, as peace with honour. At least the treaty could be improved in a progressive direction in later revisions. Lloyd George, still firmly in the saddle in Britain at a time when Wilson and Clemenceau were being undermined by domestic opposition, was uniquely placed to make this possible over the next few years.

The main consequence of the Paris peace conference on Lloyd George's premiership was to make foreign affairs the major priority of his remaining years in office, to the partial neglect of affairs in Britain and in Ireland. So many unresolved questions were left to fester in relation to Germany, let alone Austria and Turkey (with whom peace was not concluded until the Lausanne treaty in 1923 after Lloyd George had fallen from power) that he was deeply immersed in his role as international peacemaker. For a brief moment, Britain and its prime minister seemed to enjoy a unique initiative in dictating the new pattern of post-war Europe. A score of peace conferences culminating in the failure at Genoa in April to May 1922 tried to follow up this initiative. To the extent that he had a unique commitment in the international sphere, Lloyd George's contact with the political scene at home became more remote. For this reason, critics like Northcliffe alleged that he was neglecting his domestic obligations, and becoming far too Olympian and detached a figure. In addition, it may be surmised that the pattern of events at Paris and the summit diplomacy that followed it, served to reinforce Lloyd George's liking for the presidential style. He dominated conferences by force of personality and quickness of mind. His personal aides like Philip Kerr bypassed the official civil servants of the Foreign Office or the Treasury. Old weapons like the press were freely used in the pursuit of Lloyd Georgian diplomacy, with all its bewildering twists and turns. From this arose, in part, his long feud with Northcliffe's *Times*, whose successive editors, Geoffrey Dawson and Wickham Steed, relentlessly criticised Britain's post-war foreign policy from a right-wing, nationalist stance. In general, Lloyd George's absorption with foreign affairs strengthened his love of instant decision-making rather than for the laborious routine channels of parliamentary government. It strengthened his determination that a prime minister must govern, free from the restraints imposed by political parties or pressure groups. Through his role in international diplomacy he furthered his aim of developing a new style of national leadership at home, building on the base of the wartime premiership.

Even so, freed from the Paris peace conference in July 1919, Lloyd George had no option but to return to the home front. Here again his activity and energy were remarkable. His government after all was a broad-based coalition, including Unionists, Liberals, a few Labour men and mavericks like Milner. Its unifying force was the prime minister himself. Without him, it had no reason for continuing its existence. Once he returned to the domestic scene, Lloyd George strove to give it relevance and life. He focused his attention on a wide

range of issues, intervening freely in departmental matters, or doing so through advisers like Kerr or Edward Grigg. On agriculture, on housing, inevitably on Welsh affairs (for instance in pushing through disestablishment of the Church in August 1919) Lloyd George acted as a kind of minister of all departments. He was not averse to intervening on both sides of a controversial issue as he did with the Anti-Dumping Bill of 1921 which threatened free trade. Minister after minister voiced anxiety over the prime minister's interference in departmental affairs. There was the unspoken fear of Caesarism, of dictatorship. When the Cabinet had to meet in Inverness Town Hall in September 1921, to accommodate the prime minister's holiday in the Scottish highlands at that time, it seemed to emphasise his domination, almost to the point of parody. Yet without him the ministry would collapse. Certainly there was no conceivable rival in sight.

ABOVE AND RIGHT Lloyd George relaxing on his holiday at Gairloch in the Scottish highlands in 1921.

In three areas of policy, his interventions in detailed areas of policy were especially notable – labour, Ireland and foreign affairs. In dealing with organised labour he took on a vast personal burden. He regarded himself as having a proven expertise in labour relations, especially since his period at the Board of Trade. The British trade unions, especially in the mining and railway industries, were in militant mood in 1919 to 1921. Strikes multiplied; class tension built up. Timid ministers talked of Bolshevist subversion and of possible civil war. Sir Auckland Geddes even proposed setting up loyal battalions of stockbrokers in university towns to ward off the threat of the militant workers. Violent clashes in St George's Square, Glasgow, seemed to suggest that a British revolution might not be far away. Lloyd George was not averse from using tough measures in suppressing strikes. He contemplated starving the striking railwaymen into submission in October 1919. But he

"THE CHEF."

Too many Broths don't spoil this Cook.

[May 18, 1921.]

was always anxious to provide a constructive alternative. He knew that socialism could only be countered by rational reform, not by diehard reaction or by crude red-baiting. Thus it was that he used all the formidable armoury of weapons at his disposal – delay, diplomacy and personal guile. Time and again he showed incomparable skill in handling deputations of labour leaders, and in threading together a practical compromise when none seemed to exist.

He gained his most remarkable triumph in April 1921, on 'Black Friday', when he managed to persuade, perhaps deceive, Frank Hodges, the Welsh secretary of the Miners' Federation of Great Britain, into a possible settlement on a miners' wages pool. The 'Triple Alliance' of miners, dockers and railwaymen promptly broke up. Workers' solidarity vanished like autumn leaves. Strikes markedly declined in the last eighteen months of the coalition government, and industry showed some signs of regaining confidence after the post-war slump. But 'Black Friday' proved to be a dismal day for Lloyd George's future. True, he could claim that, almost single-handed, he had averted a general strike, that he had faced the miners' demands

ABOVE Barricaded street in Glasgow in February 1919, during clashes of police and strikers.

OPPOSITE Lloyd George's personal domination over policy in the three main political issues in 1921 was clearly recognised by the cartoonists.

for nationalisation with rational, moderate proposals, that the whole range of options for running the mines was still open. More, his government had proved itself to be more than a body of diehards. It had built schools and council houses, it had introduced nation-wide unemployment insurance for the first time, it had extended social welfare benefits. With unique dexterity, Lloyd George had imposed on labour relations his own brand of firmness and of constructive reform.

On the other hand, his very dominance made him uniquely responsible for his government's labour policy. This proved to be politically damaging, especially with the increasing unemployment in the aftermath of depression in the staple industries. No longer did working men regard Lloyd George as a man of the left. Rather was he ranged with the employers as the champion of 'order' and of industrial capitalism. Workers now saw in him a man who had deceived them into sacrificing class solidarity, a man who had frustrated the new industrial democracy heralded in 1918. Even in South Wales, after the Sankey Commission, Lloyd George was a distrusted, even discredited figure amongst working men and women. By turning his premiership into an alternative Ministry of Labour, by concentrating on the de-fusing of workers' militancy, he brought a crucial phase of his political career to a close. His future decline as a popular tribune was already in the making.

Another field in which the prime minister was increasingly involved was policy towards Ireland. Here again, there was a heavy price to pay. If his industrial policies forfeited much of his working-class support, his Irish policies undermined much of his credit amongst his fellow Liberals, even those who in general supported the coalition. In 1919 and 1920 the situation in southern Ireland became more and more desperate. Irish nationalist opinion was now ranged solidly behind Sinn Fein and its demands for an Irish republic. When the Government of Ireland Act in 1920 set up a distinct parliament in Northern Ireland at Stormont, the Sinn Feiners in the south ignored it and acknowledged instead their own alternative assembly, the Dail. By the end of 1920 Ireland was engulfed in a terrifying wave of violence. The Irish Republican Army, under the command of Michael Collins, began a series of violent attacks on British positions and personnel. The new Chief Secretary for Ireland, Sir Hamar Greenwood, a Liberal ironically enough, launched a policy of overt reprisals. In addition to building up the regular British forces under Sir Nevil Macready, he also encouraged the enlistment of irregular troops, to aid the Royal

Irish Constabulary. Chief among these were the 'Black and Tans' and the 'Auxis', two para-military organisations which became notorious for their indiscipline and violence. Among the more deplorable episodes in the winter of 1920 were the burning of part of Cork by the Auxis and the indiscriminate firing into a Dublin football crowd by the Black and Tans on 'Bloody Sunday' (21 November 1920). By mid-1921 the violence had become an international scandal which severely undermined Britain's reputation abroad and sickened liberal and humanitarian opinion at home. As the British press reported, Ireland was caught up in 'a nightmare of terror'.

Until the late spring of 1921, Lloyd George himself was too absorbed in foreign affairs to devote close attention to Ireland. When he did make pronouncements, it was in warm support of the policy of armed retaliation against the IRA. The prime minister was clearly among the 'hawks' at this time. He declared against the possibility of Ireland's ever having complete independence from the British government, especially after the treasonable attitude shown by Sinn Fein during the Great War. He defended the vigorous methods used in dealing with the 'murder gang' in Ireland who were, he claimed, terrorising the Irish countryside. He seemed to draw little or no distinction between the Irish Republican Army and Sinn Fein, an essentially political body. He supported the policy of hitting back. 'We have murder by the throat,' he declared melodramatically in October 1920.

Even so he could not fail to be aware of how damaging the Irish troubles were and how they endangered his position as prime minister in several respects. It handicapped his conduct of foreign policy especially in dealing with the United States with its large Irish population concentrated in New York, Boston and other cities. It seriously undermined his reputation amongst radical and progressive opinion at home: C. P. Scott of the *Manchester Guardian*, for example, broke off all relations with Lloyd George for a time. Even the prime minister's life, no less than those of his family, was threatened, particularly after the long-drawn-out death of the Mayor of Cork, Terence MacSwiney, who went on hunger-strike for seventy-four days in protest against British government policy. The police warned that IRA assassins might strike back at the prime minister. Worst of all, Ireland now presented a frightening spectacle of lawlessness and disorder within the United Kingdom itself. The prime minister had seriously miscalculated. He had badly underestimated the strength and support of Sinn Fein in the

Ireland

ABOVE Unionist workers in a clash with Sinn Feiners in York Street, Belfast, 1920.
RIGHT Michael Collins, 'the Big Feller', leader of the IRA.

OPPOSITE 'Auxis', hated equally with the 'Black and Tans' for their violence and cruelty, holding Sinn Feiners at gun point, November 1920.

Scene outside Mountjoy Prison, Dublin, in 1920, where crowds gathered in sympathy for the hunger-strikers.

south. He had little appreciation of the problem, more familiar to us today, of subduing rural and urban guerrillas who were aided and abetted by a large segment of the civilian population.

So in the late spring of 1921 he began to involve himself much more closely in Irish affairs, and to dictate a drastic change of course. He had already been in indirect contact with Sinn Fein and its leader, Eamonn de Valera. In July, there was a break-through of a kind, and direct face-to-face discussions began at Downing Street. He managed to persuade de Valera that there existed neither in Welsh nor in Irish a word for a 'republic' and that some kind of accommodation of a free Ireland with the empire was practicable. Talks, however, almost broke down in August and not until late October did serious discussions begin with the Sinn Feiners in London. The British delegation, which included Austen Chamberlain, Lord Birkenhead, Worthington-Evans, Churchill and Greenwood, was headed by the prime minister. From the outset he dominated the discussions. In the event, it was the personal ascendancy he established over Michael Collins and Arthur Griffith, the leading Sinn Fein delegates, that turned the scale. Although Ulster was as usual an insuperable problem, it was on other issues that discussions almost foundered: on the exact nature of the relationship between a free Ireland and the British Empire; on financial and strategic issues; on the Oath of Allegiance to the Crown.

On 5 December Lloyd George resolved the deadlock in characteristic manner. Taking advantage of a private agreement he had made with Michael Collins, he threatened the remaining Irish delegates with an immediate resumption of hostilities unless they accepted the terms already agreed. Lord Longford has described the drama of the final confrontation. Lloyd George brandished two letters, one enclosing terms of an agreement, the other declaring that the Sinn Feiners refused to come within the Empire. 'Which letter am I to send? Whichever letter you choose travels by special train to Holyhead and by destroyer to Belfast. We must know your answer by ten p.m. tonight. You can have until then, but no longer, to decide whether you will give peace or war to your country.' As C.L. Mowat remarks fairly enough, Lloyd George conjured out of existence the telephone with which he could communicate to Belfast and Dublin. It was colossal bluff; all the evidence suggests that the British government and British public opinion would have been delighted to get out of southern Ireland at almost any price – but the bluff worked. Without consulting de Valera, who fortunately stayed in Dublin throughout, the Sinn Feiners were charmed into accepting unanimously the British government's terms. A month later, the treaty was narrowly endorsed (by sixty-four to fifty-seven) in the Irish Dail. The majority responded to Griffith's passionate plea: 'Is there to be no living Irish nation? Is the Irish nation to be the dead past or the prophetic future?'

All kinds of issues were left ambiguous. For the present, the six Protestant counties of Ulster were excluded from a united Ireland. This issue was left to the later adjudication of the Boundary Commission. In practice, nothing happened, the partition of Ireland continued, and Northern Ireland remained firmly in the United Kingdom for the next fifty years. Despite all the unanswered problems left in abeyance, despite the continuing violence in Ireland itself which led to fierce civil war between pro- and anti-treaty factions in 1922 to 1923, despite such appalling episodes as the murder of Field Marshal Sir

Henry Wilson in front of his home by IRA gunmen in 1922, Ireland suddenly ceased to be a major issue. It has remained essentially on the periphery of British politics ever since. The continuing violence in Northern Ireland in the period since 1969 was a tragedy for the local population. But it was no longer the central theme of British politics, while relations between Britain and the Republic of Ireland remained reasonably cordial, especially when the Fine Gael party assumed government at Dublin in 1973.

Like his handling of labour issues, Ireland shaped Lloyd George's political destiny in crucial ways. Indeed, there were those who traced the decline of the government to the upsurge of humanitarian protest against the policy of 'reprisals' in 1920 to 1921. Sir Oswald Mosley later claimed that Ireland was as fundamental a crisis of conscience for young radicals in Britain in the early 1920s as was Vietnam for young Americans in the mid-1960s. Lloyd George lost much Liberal and Labour support through his Irish policies: indeed, the pressure of public opinion on his left flank played its part in driving him to the negotiation table. His support of the indiscriminate reprisals in southern Ireland was a disheartening episode, the darkest chapter of his entire career. On the other hand, he did bring peace to Ireland in the end. He accorded a greater measure of freedom to the twenty-six southern counties than even Parnell had ever demanded. He could claim to be the man who had solved the Irish question where Pitt, Peel and Gladstone had all failed. In practice, he lost more support from those who felt that his policies had been too lenient and that in the end it had led to abject surrender in the face of Irish gunmen. As right-wing critics argued, direct action brought results where fifty years of constitutional pressure at Westminster had failed. Unionist support for the government was seriously compromised by the Irish treaty negotiations. Bonar Law himself went through agonies of conscience, in view of his close connection with Ulster Unionism. Rank-and-file Unionists protested against the betrayal of sacred pledges to the southern Unionists and to imperial unity. It seemed to symbolise all that was unacceptable about Lloyd George's premiership. This alienation of much of his right flank led directly to his decline and fall in 1922.

For the rest, his main preoccupation, as has been seen, was with foreign affairs. Throughout 1920 and 1921, he was largely concerned with trying to restore the political and economic fabric of Europe after the partial settlement of Versailles. In a

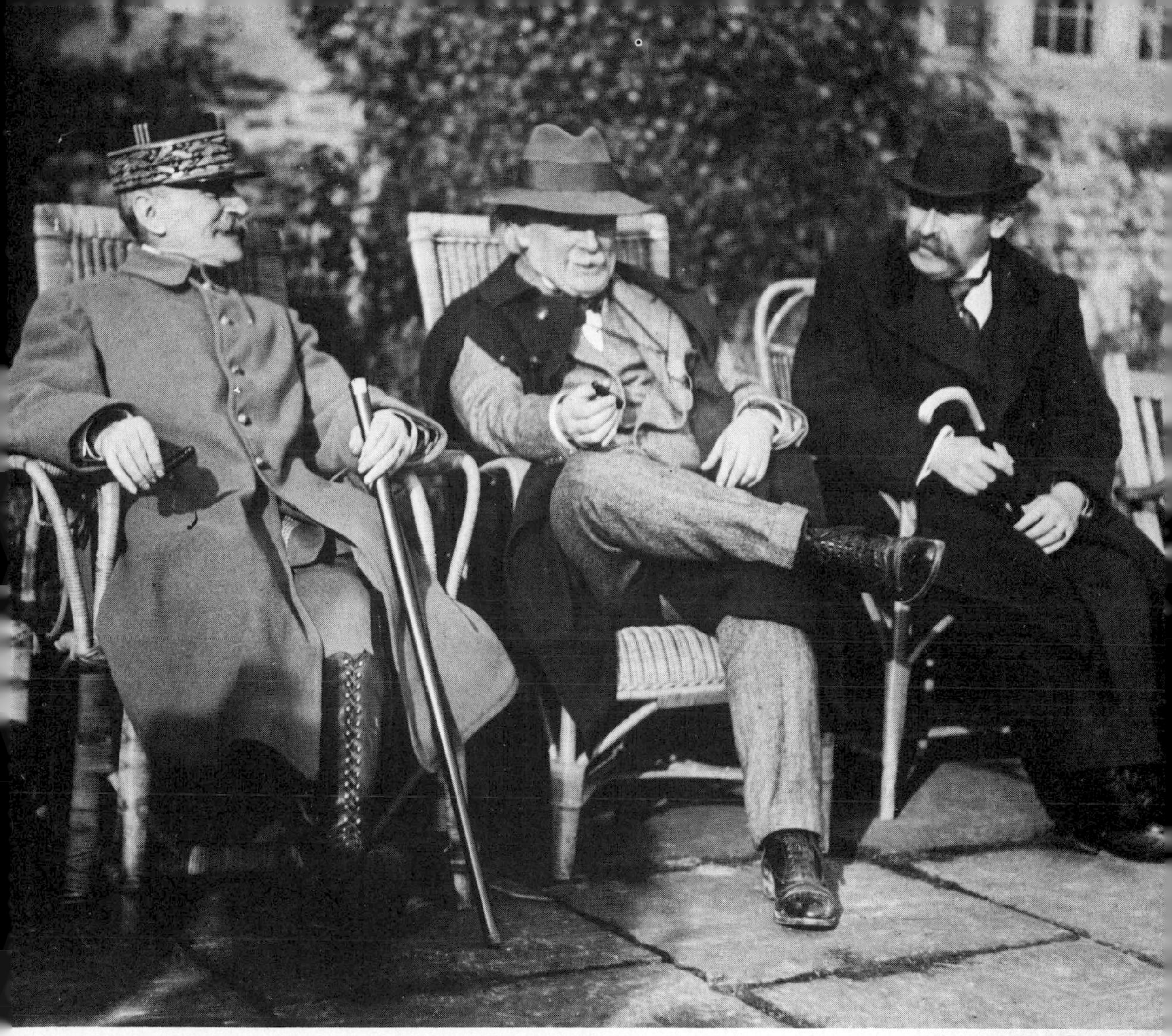

sequence of international conferences, he was the dominant figure. Even with Lord Curzon, 'that most superior person', succeeding the more pliant Balfour at the Foreign Office, Lloyd George continued to set the pace for British diplomacy. Curzon was bullied into weeping submission. In the full glare of international publicity, Lloyd George tried to construct a new framework for relations between the nations. No one was better equipped to handle summit diplomacy than he was, with his genius for assimilating vital facts and for captivating an audience, with his marvellous sense of atmosphere, his talent for knowing when to threaten, when to beguile. Now as ever it was truly said of him that 'he could charm a bird off a bough'. In the 'conference era' that led up to Genoa in April 1922 his presence lent a vital momentum to international negotiations.

On the other hand, his intuitive methods and circular

Briand, the French premier, Lloyd George and Marshal Foch at a weekend conference at Chequers in 1921.

THE WORLD'S PREMIER DUETTISTS.

The Welsh Harp. " You won't take this piece too *furioso,* will you, dear boy ? "
The French Horn. " Certainly not, *mon brave ;* not if you don't take it too *moderato.*"

[January 26, 1921.]

approaches, circumventing the conventional channels of diplomacy, could lead to serious mistakes, and to inadequate preparation. A short-term bargain struck in an emotional atmosphere one hectic evening could fade away in the cold light of the following morning. The Genoa conference was to show the dangers of too flamboyant and over-confident an approach to the subtle mysteries of diplomacy. Further, his instinct about people could lead him astray. The personality of Venizelos, the Greek prime minister to whom he felt especially drawn, played its part in leading Lloyd George into an attempted dismemberment of the Turkish empire which was to cost him dear – indeed to drive him from office. At least it could be claimed that Lloyd George alone tried, however erratically, to seize the initiative in the storm-tossed world of 1919 to 1922. Alone of the major peacemakers in 1919 he attempted that serious revision of the peace treaties without which stability was impossible.

OPPOSITE Cartoon of Lloyd George and Briand, 1921. Lloyd George battled to secure a constructive settlement for Europe, and particularly to moderate the French attitude to reparations from Germany.

His objectives throughout this period were clear enough: conciliation and recovery. He wound up, after some equivocal shifts and turns, the allied intervention in Russia. By April 1920, the last British troops had been evacuated. He strove hard to bring the new Bolshevik régime into the comity of nations. An Anglo-Russian trade treaty was signed in March 1921. Diehards like Churchill, bent on an anti-communist crusade, were slapped down. The premier tried also to normalise relations with Germany and to scale down reparation payments at Spa, San Remo and elsewhere. At the Cannes conference in January 1922, he was very close to reconciling a moderate financial settlement with Germany with a permanent inter-allied guarantee of the eastern frontiers of France to compensate. The whole pact seemed to be agreed with Briand, the French premier, during a celebrated game of golf at Cannes. But the scene revived all the Anglophobe prejudice of the French press and politicians. Briand had to return to Paris, where he was driven from office. The right-wing nationalist Poincaré, a Lorrainer with a fierce hatred of Germany, succeeded him as prime minister, and the hope of a positive accord with the German government vanished at once. Soon the two great outcast countries, Germany and Russia, were to come to terms in a secret treaty at Rapallo in April 1922, on the eve of the Genoa conference, thus confirming one of Lloyd George's secret fears.

Lloyd George's other objective was economic recovery. He sought to end the chaos over war debts and reparations, to restore trade with central and eastern Europe by use of long-

The famous golf game at Cannes, January 1922, during which Lloyd George and Briand at last reached agreement on terms. Briand's immediate downfall from office made this very short-lived.

term credits, to rebuild Britain's position as the arbiter of the gold standard and the major money market of the world. He was deeply concerned at the rise of unemployment in Britain, and anxious to find new markets abroad and to stabilise currencies based on gold. At Genoa in April and May 1922 he attempted a package deal which would secure all these commercial and financial aims, including the *de facto* recognition of Soviet Russia as a preliminary to reviving trade with eastern Europe. But all his objectives eluded him. Plagued by hostile reporting in much of the British and French press, notably in Northcliffe's *Times* where the editor, Wickham Steed, pursued a mischievous campaign of misrepresentation, Lloyd George

Balfour and Lloyd George seated aside Briand's successor, Poincaré, the right-wing nationalist with a passionate hatred of Germany.

saw the discussions founder in the face of French intransigence. As has been seen, Russia and Germany were virtually isolated from the start after the Rapallo treaty; the attempted recognition of Russia came to nothing; moves to try to achieve commercial recovery in the succession states in central Europe failed utterly. After three years of endeavour to try to establish international affairs on a basis of harmonious interdependence rather than on vengeance, Lloyd George could only show a record of noble failure. The insecurity of the international scene in the remaining period up to 1939 was already foreshadowed.

As with his labour and Irish policies, Lloyd George's ventures in foreign affairs affected his position as prime minister in a damaging fashion. The aloof, presidential method with which he conducted conferences, making free use of the Cabinet Office and the Garden Suburb encouraged all the fears of his desire for dictatorship. Labour and Liberal critics attacked him for truckling to anti-German sentiment in France, and endeavouring to sustain the secret treaties and 'the system of Versailles'. In dealing with the Turkish empire in the Near East, he was accused of being more interested in oil-bearing Arabs than in Greek Christians. More damagingly, in view of his government's dependence on Tory votes, he was attacked from the right for giving way to sentimental liberalism. The anti-German hysteria of the 'coupon election' was still rampant. It emerged anew when Unionist supporters of the government rose up in protest against attempts to conciliate the Bolshevists in Russia. In March 1922, Churchill, Birkenhead and other ministers led a successful revolt against the premier's attempt to secure agreement to the *de facto* recognition of Russia. The whole episode was deeply harmful to Lloyd George's position. Sir Edward Grigg thought that three-quarters of the Cabinet were now disloyal to him. But there was still a long way to go between disgruntled protest and all-out revolt. To the public at large, Lloyd George's dazzling prominence in international diplomacy helped to add to his magnetism at home. It seemed that 'the man who won the war' could also pose with some justice as the bringer of peace.

Whether he could remain in office much longer, though, depended not on the remote peaks of summit diplomacy, but on the obscure foothills of party politics. He had, after all, no firm party base. He was still at the mercy, at least in theory, of the Unionists. His only real hope of a long-term future, then, rested on his creating a new foundation of support. The prime minister was news: he dominated the headlines and the news photographs; he received the freedom of cities galore. But, without humble workers in the constituencies, he had no lasting future. The premiership he was creating would dissolve as had the war that provided the need for it.

There were only two possibilities now. One was to create a new 'Coalition' party on a national basis, to give the Coalition government an enduring form. The other was to make the Coalition between Unionists and Coalition Liberals a permanent alliance. In late 1919 and early 1920 Lloyd George devoted time and resource to following up the former objective. He sought a Centre Party. He argued that the old issues of pre-war politics – free trade, church-and-chapel rivalries, land reform, the drink question and the rest – had passed into the history books. An up-to-date National Party should be formed to accord with the new mood. It would steer a middle course between the diehards and the socialists (indeed, anti-socialism was a dominant theme in Lloyd George's speeches at this time, culminating in his making a comparison between Arthur Henderson and Lenin). A new supra-party government, underpinned by constituency machines, could pursue the supreme objectives of reconstruction at home and abroad. It was somewhat along the lines of his abortive Coalition plan of 1910, save that social reform loomed less large than before.

But again party defeated him. Very reluctantly, Bonar Law and the Unionists agreed to a 'fusion' of the two main Coalition parties. But it was always a fragile plant, and it

WHAT'S IN A NAME ?

Mate. "While we *are* doin' her up, what about givin' her a new name ? How would 'Fusion' do ?"

Captain. "'Fusion' or 'Confusion'—it's all one to me so long as I'm skipper."

[March 24, 1920.]

An apt cartoon of Lloyd George's attempt to find a firm party backing by creating a new 'fusion' party from Unionists and Coalition Liberals.

A DOWNING STREET MELODRAMA.

The Premier. "Come on in, Bonar; I love these fancy blood-curdlers. Best tonic in the world."

[February 4, 1920.]

By February 1920 Lloyd George's political position was precarious in the extreme, despite his confident front.

withered away when in March 1920 the Coalition Liberals unexpectedly turned it down. Liberals in the government and in the House feared the sacrifice of age-old Liberal principles like free trade; they still dreamed of Liberal reunion. Lloyd George's new red-baiting rhetoric suggested that the 'fusion' party would be strongly right-wing, and that the old humane traditions of British Liberalism would be submerged. The only Coalition Liberal minister, apart from Lloyd George, really committed to the idea of 'fusion' was Churchill. He sought a more effective instrument with which to defeat the Red Peril – to continue his anti-labour policies first implemented when troops were sent to Tonypandy in 1910. The Liberals, apart from him, threw the idea of fusion out. The Unionists then lost interest in it too. From that time onwards, Lloyd George's political position in real terms, however glamorous his role in international and national affairs, was precarious in the extreme. He still had no firm party backing. He was losing support rapidly among Liberal voters; Labour voters had rejected him long since. His main associates now were businessmen, captains of industry, press lords, instead of rank-and-file Liberals. 'He has completely changed,' lamented Lord Riddell. Lloyd George's yearning for a new mode of higher politics, resounding to the smack of firm government, seemed to have corrupted his judgement.

The other political tactic for perpetuating his government – a permanent alliance of Unionists and Coalition Liberals – had even less hope of success. The Coalition Liberals turned themselves into a distinct party in early 1922, after much heart-searching, and cut themselves adrift from their Asquithian comrades. But it scarcely seemed worth the Unionists' while to ally with them now. As the prime minister declined in public esteem, the 'Coaly Libs' seemed a very weak link in the government. They were losing ground in by-elections in Wales and elsewhere. On the other hand, Unionist party workers, rallying behind their chairman, Sir George Younger, felt their confidence returning. No longer did Lloyd George seem indispensable. The best he could hope for was a continuance of the alliance with the Unionists until after the next general election. Until then, he would continue to preside shakily over an increasingly right-wing administration. After that his future was totally obscure. More and more he seemed an accidental survivor of the war years, a coalitionist in the revived world of party. Quite simply he appeared out of date.

It was in early 1921 that the first clear signs appeared that Lloyd George was beginning to lose control of his administration. It would be wrong to be too dogmatic about this. Most of the evidence still suggests that until midsummer of 1922 most of his supporters still felt that in the short run the prime minister had to be retained, for all his faults. Despite a ferocious campaign against him in the press, despite his becoming the unique target of the government's unpopularity, he retained wide public support to the end. One surmises that had Gallup Polls existed in those years a majority of the public would have continued to declare their confidence in their prime minister, at least until September 1922.

What was crucial, though, was Lloyd George's support at

Austen Chamberlain who succeeded Bonar Law as Unionist leader.

Whitehall and at Westminster. Here there were disturbing symptoms. It was now becoming clear that he was having difficulty in retaining control of his Cabinet. This became more marked after March 1921 when Bonar Law resigned on grounds of ill-health. His successor as Unionist leader, Austen Chamberlain, quite failed to maintain Law's calm ascendancy over the backbenchers. As a result, Unionist criticism of policy within the Cabinet became more vocal. One easy target of ministerial criticism was the role played by Lloyd George's cadre of personal aides, especially his private army of advisers in the Garden Suburb. Gradually, the intrusion of the prime minister's secretaries into public affairs was cut back. A major change was the resignation of Philip Kerr in March 1921 to run the pro-government Liberal newspaper, the *Daily Chronicle*. Lloyd George's ascendancy over his Cabinet was now harder to maintain. Its Liberal elements were gradually being eased out.

Addison went in July 1921 after a row with his chief about the financial mismanagement of the housing programme. Montagu followed in March 1922 after a fierce attack on the prime minister's dictatorial tactics and his policy towards Turkey. The result was that the Cabinet was increasingly the prey to a newly confident right-wing Unionism, backed up by the even more right-wing Churchill, which Lloyd George found hard indeed to control.

His authority over parliament was also being whittled away. Attacks on the government by backbench Unionists, accusing the government of craven peace-mongering, in India, Ireland, Russia and elsewhere, continued to mount. They did not hesitate to exploit anti-semitism against Jewish Liberal ministers like Mond and Montagu. They were backed up by an irresponsible campaign whipped up in the press, by Horatio Bottomley among others, which accused the government of wasteful expenditure on housing and the social services. In themselves, these attacks were not difficult to handle, even though they drew attention to Lloyd George's lengthy absences from the House during international conferences. But the Unionist critics received a bonus when Bonar Law unexpectedly recovered his health sufficiently to return to the House in late 1921. Even though he continued to protest his loyalty to the government, his very presence gave encouragement to the critics. It meant that there was, in theory at least, an alternative prime minister to hand, should the Unionist protesters break out in rebellion.

It was in the sphere of party politics that Lloyd George was most vulnerable. He had no party base. He had forfeited almost all Labour support. The Coalition Liberals were shattered in morale: some of them were drifting over to reunite with the Asquithians, now reviving in confidence after recent by-election victories (including Asquith's own return at Paisley). Still the 'Coaly Libs' had really no other path to follow except servile support of the prime minister. The most damaging aspect of the party scene was the disaffection of so many rank-and-file Unionists up and down the country. Particularly after the Irish treaty in December 1921, which seemed to many Unionists a deplorable surrender to terrorism, Unionist constituency workers unleashed a torrent of complaint against the Coalition. They yearned for independence and urged Austen Chamberlain, their leader, to free them from their dependence on the mercurial Welsh premier. They now found a formidable spokesman in the Unionist party chairman, Sir George

Younger. A remarkable episode took place in January 1922 when Lloyd George sought to dissolve parliament to exploit the interest taken in the recent conference at Cannes. Younger publicly announced that the Tory rank-and-file would not agree; it would, he claimed, split the party from top to bottom. Austen Chamberlain had no alternative but to agree. Shortly afterwards, Bonar Law, who had been approached through the mediation of Beaverbrook, declined to rejoin the government. As a result of these twin blows, Lloyd George was unable to dissolve parliament. He was deprived of one of the basic weapons of any prime minister – the right to call a general election. The signs of impending downfall were never clearer.

Throughout the first half of 1922 the position of the government became increasingly difficult. There were innumerable crises which Lloyd George – like a 'beetle in a glass case' as he wearily described himself – had somehow to surmount. The continuing violence in Ireland was one point of friction with the Unionists. The murder of Field Marshal Sir Henry Wilson by IRA gunmen launched off a furious barrage of protest against the government's surrender to Sinn Fein. As has been seen, Lloyd George's attempt to gain his Cabinet's agreement to the recognition of Soviet Russia in March 1922 led him into another desperate passage. The prime minister seemed a more and more lonely figure. His domestic life with Dame Margaret (as she now was) was largely a matter of form. With the assistance of Frances Stevenson, he was now setting up a new country home for himself in Churt, in Surrey. His enemies, especially in the press, were more savage and unrelenting than ever.

There was one consolation, at least: the resignation of Northcliffe from ownership of *The Times*, and shortly afterwards his death. Lloyd George's most implacable enemy in the press world had finally been removed. This led to a remarkable venture, an attempt to make the prime minister proprietor – perhaps even editor – of *The Times*; but the plan came to nothing. Lloyd George had few close advisers to assist or console him in the face of the attacks from his opponents. Men like Hankey and Thomas Jones were basically civil servants: indeed, the latter was already mending his fences with Bonar Law in case of a defeat of the government. The cadre of personal advisers, headed by Kerr, was dissolving, with the more disreputable elements like Sir William Sutherland surviving. None of the Cabinet was in any sense an intimate colleague. Isolated in the centre of the stage, Lloyd George was the most wide open of targets, and critics from the ILP to

Lloyd George and Dame Margaret at Criccieth, 1922. Their marriage by this time was under strain.

Horatio Bottomley launched indiscriminate attacks upon him.

The prime minister's decline was accelerated by two temporary issues that loomed unexpectedly large in the politics of early 1922. One was the 'anti-waste' campaign already referred to, and given new momentum by Addison's failures in managing the finances of the housing programme. This led to the notorious report of the committee under Sir Eric Geddes early in 1922 which recommended almost one hundred million pounds in economies. Housing, education and the social services bore the brunt of these cuts: the welfare state took decades to recover. The government's relative impotence in the face of a well-managed scare campaign in the right-wing press was amply confirmed.

More harmful still was the festering scandal of the Lloyd George Fund. This arose directly from the prime minister's unusual position in lacking organised party support. In particular, he was short of money, since the Liberal machinery and party funds were still in the hands of the Asquithian organisers.

Lloyd George, then, had somehow to try to amass by private means the funds without which his political future would be doomed. Through private donations, mostly obtained by the trading of honours and other political patronage, Captain Freddie Guest, the government's Liberal whip, was able to build up a mighty fund which eventually reached at least three million pounds. A particularly active associate in these operations was Sir William Sutherland who, it was alleged, 'traded baronetcies and peerages' in London's clubland. According to one source, twelve thousand pounds for a knighthood and thirty-five thousand pounds for a baronetcy were the going rates. Soon these unusual arrangements were being given wide currency by Unionist critics of the government. There was in

THE ROAD TO ECONOMY.

The Shepherd. "I wonder if any of you sheep could show me the way."

["Let the Nation set the example (in economy) to the Government."—*Mr. Lloyd George.*]

[December 8, 1920.]

Cartoon of December 1920 underlining the lack of public confidence in Lloyd George's handling of the alleged 'waste' in public spending.

fact a peculiar flavour of humbug about many of these charges. The trading of honours for political purposes had gone on for fifty years, even under Gladstone. What was the difference between the sale of honours for an established party like the Conservatives and for a new one like the Coalition Liberals? In any case, Lloyd George could point out that, at first, the Unionists took fifty per cent of the proceeds of any funds that were going. He himself dismissed the charges about the sale of peerages with contempt. Never a man overwhelmed with respect for the House of Lords, it mattered little to him whether a man gained a peerage by the accident of birth or by recent political services. The only difference between his practice and that of previous prime ministers in relation to peerages was that Lloyd George created rather more of them. Whether the intellectual or social standards of the Upper House were diminished, whether the currency of titles was debased or not, were of no concern to Wales's Great Commoner. Nor could it be claimed that the money in the fund went to line Lloyd George's own pocket. It went to political purposes. The prime minister, until he sold the fund's shareholding in United Newspapers in 1928, was still a comparatively poor man by the standards of most politicians of the time. Later on he produced a more subtle defence of his methods. It was better to sell honours than to sell principles. The Conservative and Labour Parties were dictated to, through receiving contributions from financial and industrial pressure groups, such as the brewers and the trade unions. Selling titles was a far cleaner method of raising money.

Still, the outcry against the 'honours scandal' is not so easily dismissed, even when the political motives behind it are discounted. The creation of a large private fund, never submitted to public audit, as a personal war chest was a breach with the canons of political morality. It was understandable that the big battalions should distrust the Welsh freebooter, particularly when he used such corrupt intermediaries as Maundy Gregory, the lapsed son of a Southampton clergyman (whom Bonar Law and Baldwin also employed). There was also the damaging political point that the fund directed attention in the most embarrassing way to Lloyd George's personal position. It emphasised the way in which he was flouting the conventions of public life. The taint of corruption added a more unsavoury aspect to the record of the Coalition government. In the face of a public outcry, notably by the outraged peers themselves, Lloyd George had to appoint a committee of inquiry. Privately, he admitted that some recent creations, such as conferring a title on Joseph Robinson, a South African millionaire of dubious reputation, had been careless. Robinson had been recently criticised in the High Court for making illicit profits in South African mining companies, and for defrauding shareholders. In the face of such cases as this, it is not surprising that the mud thrown at the prime minister by critics of his fund continued to stick. The glittering millions he had hoarded remained to weigh him down, fatally, for the remainder of his life.

Nevertheless, for a brief and deceptive moment in the later summer of 1922, the government seemed to have won a brief respite. For a time Ireland was peaceful, the labour scene free from strikes, the economy marginally reviving. The Washington Naval Treaty seemed to presage a world finally at peace. Lloyd George, at appalling cost to his physical and nervous resources, was still in command of his administration. The swelling army of Unionist critics still lacked a leader more substantial than Brigadier Page-Croft, while the Asquithians were of little account. The critics to some degree were being thinned out. Northcliffe was dead; Horatio Bottomley was in gaol; Colonel Repington had been involved in renewed marital scandal. Even after the torrents of abuse which he had endured, Lloyd George was far from helpless. On the contrary, he was still able to look forward to a general election in the autumn, still in harness with the Unionists, in which the country would be invited again to return Lloyd George as the architect of peace and stability.

Suddenly, his entire position collapsed. In late August, a crisis blew up in Asia Minor. The Turks under Mustapha Kemal smashed through the Greek position, sacked Smyrna with immense loss of life, and advanced towards the British-held position at Chanak on the Dardanelles. Lloyd George had long pursued a dangerous policy in this theatre. From his earliest years in politics, he had a finely developed contempt for the Turks. He regarded them as indeed 'unspeakable', a race unfitted to rule. Kemal was merely 'a carpet-seller in a bazaar'. Lloyd George had given the Greeks under Venizelos every encouragement to invade Asia Minor, and at the Treaty of Sèvres in 1920 had tried to carve up the Turkish dominions. Not all the Unionist members of the Cabinet shared Lloyd George's violently anti-Turkish views. But even they mostly agreed with him that it was vital to secure British control over the Dardanelles and thereby of the eastern Mediterranean. The traditions of Gladstone and of Disraeli for once coincided.

Mustapha Kemal, the Turkish leader whom Lloyd George dismissed contemptuously as 'a carpet-seller in a bazaar'.

In this final crisis, however, Lloyd George's position was revealed as fundamentally weak. No major European state would back him up in the event of war with Turkey. The French would do nothing, and their prime minister, Poincaré, was widely believed to be giving secret encouragement to Mustapha Kemal. The Italians would provide no assistance either. Nor would the Empire help Britain in this crisis. MacKenzie King, the Liberal premier of Canada, made it very plain that Britain's problems in the eastern Mediterranean were no concern of Canada. In any case, he was annoyed that Churchill's request for assistance from the Empire had, owing to a miscalculation of the time difference between Britain and North America, been published in the press before he had received it. Australia would do nothing either, while South Africa offered no reply at all. Only New Zealand would offer a battalion in assistance. It was an interesting index of how feeble imperial unity really was.

Most crucial of all, it became increasingly apparent that

British public opinion, still weary after years of war and now taught by Keynes how pointless and unjust had been the settlement that followed it, would not support war against Turkey. Many wondered how important this region was to British national security anyhow. Labour and Liberal spokesmen condemned Lloyd George for war-mongering. True, in the Cabinet, Unionist ministers – even Birkenhead – rallied to Lloyd George's support; while Churchill, previously a critic of policy towards Turkey, warmed to the prospect of a good fight and was anxious to dispatch battleships to pound the enemy into submission. On the other hand, several Unionist ministers, including Curzon, Peel, Griffith-Boscawen and the still relatively obscure President of the Board of Trade, Stanley Baldwin, made vocal their anxiety about war with Turkey. Resignations were threatened by several Unionist junior ministers. In the party's rank-and-file up and down the country, there were vehement criticisms of Lloyd George's conduct of British diplomacy and methods of government in general. All this might not have mattered had the critics suddenly not found a leader, almost by default. On 7 October *The Times* published a letter by Bonar Law on the Turkish crisis. While he endorsed the government's handling of the issue in general terms, he added some damaging observations about the futility of Britain alone trying to act 'as policeman of the world'. This chimed in with the new isolationist mood of the post-war era. However much Bonar Law might disavow it, he had given the underground Unionist revolt the lift it needed. Several junior ministers were in open rebellion. Curzon, the Foreign Secretary, who had for years endured slights and rebuffs from the prime minister, seemed about to follow them. At a private meeting with Lloyd George on 9 October, arranged by Beaverbrook, Bonar Law urged the prime minister to resign and to dissolve the Coalition. Lloyd George himself, seemingly oblivious to the crisis, deliberately went out of his way to provoke his critics in a speech at Manchester on 14 October in which he made scathing attacks on the Turks. He also made a memorable onslaught on an Asquithian critic, Viscount Gladstone – 'the finest living embodiment of the Liberal principle that talent is not hereditary'. But the time for rhetorical triumphs had passed.

In desperation, Austen Chamberlain, the Unionist leader, called a meeting of Unionist members of parliament in the Carlton Club for the morning of 19 October. The purpose was to slap down the dissidents and make the party agree to a new general election to be fought on a coalition basis. But Chamberlain was always a maladroit politician and he had miscalculated fatally. The mood of rebellion was too widespread. The rank-and-file Unionists had had more than enough of Lloyd George; they had now found a popular issue on which to throw him out. They were given last minute encouragement by the news of a by-election at Newport, Monmouthshire, in which an independent Unionist, Clarry, defeated both the Liberal and Labour candidates. Most crucial of all, in an agonising discussion with Beaverbrook on the evening of 18 October, Bonar Law made up his mind that he would declare publicly against the Coalition the following morning, to restore Unionist party unity. The debate at the Carlton Club the next day followed a predictable course. Almost all the Unionist ministers – Austen Chamberlain, Birkenhead, Balfour, Horne, Worthington-Evans, Lee of Fareham – spoke in favour of the need to keep the Coalition in being. They declared that they could not follow the party into the unknown hazards of independence. A revolt now might mean a Unionist schism as serious as that suffered by the Liberals in 1918. But Bonar Law's influence outweighed all of these. The most dramatic intervention was made by Stanley Baldwin, who spoke with rare passion. He denounced Lloyd George as 'a dynamic force', and a dynamic force, Baldwin characteristically added, was 'a very terrible thing'. Somehow this simple utterance seemed to sum up years of pent-up resentment endured by the party regulars during the Lloyd George Coalition. By 185 votes to 88, the Unionists voted down the Coalition. Lloyd George received the news in Frances Stevenson's office. He knew what it meant. Later that day he resigned office.

His last act as prime minister was to parody – to cheer up his demoralised personal advisers – his return to Downing Street as the head of a deputation to demand grants for Welsh education from a future prime minister. His wife, still attached somehow to him and his future, had to clear up the mess and find somewhere to live. (For a time they lived in a flat in London rented from Sir Edward Grigg.) Lloyd George's premiership had collapsed in the same unorthodox way in which it had been launched. He had suffered the rarest of fates for a modern prime minister – defeat at the hands of his own parliamentary supporters. The party regulars had gained belated revenge for 1916 over the Welsh outsider.

Lloyd George's position as a peacetime prime minister seems in retrospect to have been so precarious that it is easy to dismiss

Lloyd George moving out of 10 Downing Street in October 1922.

it as a freakish interlude. From his return from Versailles, his premiership seems to have been punctuated by such a bizarre sequence of crises that his tenure of office until October 1922 appears as a feat of political escapology without parallel in recent history, one worthy of Houdini himself. Certainly, Lloyd George's political weakness at home is beyond dispute. Since the failure of the 'fusion' scheme in March 1920 he had no clear way ahead. He had no party support and was to some considerable degree the prisoner of events. He drifted erratically from moves to reunite with the Asquithians to dreams of a new super-party in which progressive Unionists, National Liberals and patriotic Labour would form a permanent majority and transcend the petty party squabbles of the past. Until 19 October 1922 these dreams never had tangible substance, and in retrospect his fall seems to have been preordained.

On the other hand, too much should not be allowed to hindsight. At least until the summer of 1922, Lloyd George was central to every political calculation. After all, the Labour Party was still far from being a party of government: it still largely resembled a trade union pressure group of an essentially defensive character. The Independent Liberals could never gain office on their own. The Coalition could provide shelter to all those Unionists fearful of bolshevism, apprehensive of striking out on their own after being out of office on an independent basis since 1905. The later experience of Baldwin at the 1923 general election showed how well founded some of these Unionist fears were. To some extent, then, Lloyd George could survive and prosper because of the continuing weakness of his rivals, and because each of the groups supporting him found him to be in some sense indispensable. In addition, it should not be forgotten how fearful men were when confronted with the new challenges of the post-war era. In particular, organised labour conjured up nameless terrors in the minds of the orthodox. In the face of such socialist demands as a capital levy, the appeal of a national government more than nullified criticisms of 'anti-waste' or the 'honours scandal'. In this strange new world, Lloyd George, the proven leader during the crisis of total war, was the one tower of refuge now. So it seemed until the final collapse over Chanak.

What kind of a government was the post-war Coalition? Historians have lately pointed out that many of the charges launched against it were unjust. It was in many ways a government of moderation and reform. It sought peace in foreign affairs; it promoted naval disarmament; it ended turmoil in Ireland; it partly pacified India; it de-fused labour unrest; it passed a widespread programme of social reform until the impact of the Geddes axe. For a government widely supposed to be dependent on hard-faced reactionaries who had lined their pockets during the war, it was not an unimpressive record. Much of it was the direct, almost single-handed, achievement of the prime minister. An honourable observer like Scott of the *Manchester Guardian* admitted after Lloyd George's resignation that, even taking into account such dark passages as the retaliatory policies in Ireland, the government had been one that Liberals could endorse without shame.

More significant in the present context, though, is the importance of the peacetime Coalition in shaping the office of the prime minister. Here it is clear that it did not leave any lasting impression on the machinery of government. The main innovations like the Cabinet Office had been creations of war. Other instruments like the Garden Suburb in its more extended peacetime role did not long survive. Lloyd George's imperious methods, his deliberate flouting of parliamentary convention made a strong premiership on a permanent basis all the harder to maintain. Succeeding prime ministers, at least until Neville Chamberlain's premiership in 1937, took a much more modest view of their roles. Baldwin and MacDonald, indeed, regarded themselves as representing reactions against the Lloyd George era, purging public life of the improprieties of the 1918 to 1922 period. Bonar Law had already abolished the Garden Suburb and nothing like it later emerged. The truth was that, while much had changed in the economic, social and cultural make-up of Britain since 1914, the dead weight of political convention, based on party, parliament, Cabinet government and the civil service, was still overwhelming. Once the war emergency passed, Lloyd George's style of leadership became redundant. Supra-party aides like Kerr became irrelevant. Just as businessmen hankered for the pre-war world of the gold standard and the supremacy of the City, so politicians longed for the 'normalcy' of the world they had lost.

The results were far-reaching. While other nations were to experiment with powerful executives, even with dictatorships, Lloyd George's ascendancy had ensured that in Britain parliament and party would continue to serve as checks on the central government. The results were full of ironies. The greatest democrat of his day, Lloyd George had helped to ensure the discredit of strong democratic government. The tribune of popular radicalism, he had so divided and tormented the British Left as to leave the Conservatives in a position of unprecedented dominance. The apostle of the politics of action, he left Britain unwittingly a prey to passivity and complacency during the locust years that followed his downfall. Gloomily meditating on his fate, the old tragedian, still only fifty-nine, retired to the wings to his new life at Churt.

6

THE WIZARD IN THE WINGS

1922-45

AFTER his fall from power in October 1922 Lloyd George was never to come significantly near to gaining power again. At the general election which followed two months later, he made little impact, even though the crowds that flocked to hear his speeches were as immense and enthusiastic as ever. He finished up with only fifty-seven 'National Liberal' supporters, in a political limbo of his own. Within two months, he had been dashed down from the pinnacle of power. The remaining period of his life, until his death in March 1945, saw no permanent recovery.

For those concerned with Lloyd George as a prime minister, these later years raise two main issues. First, how was it that his overwhelming dominance in the years 1916 to 1922 was followed by such a comparatively minor role in politics in this last phase? And secondly, what survived, in his outlook and methods, from the years in Downing Street? How far were his objectives after 1922 simply a consequence of his assumptions and experiences while prime minister?

With regard to the first of these issues, it is clear that the politics of the 1920s were in large measure a reaction against Lloyd George, a reaction in which the Conservative and Labour parties made common cause. Lloyd George's personal ascendancy, given added edge by the personal flavour of the Lloyd George Fund, had provoked resentment on all sides. When Bonar Law retired as prime minister in July 1923, to die shortly afterwards, he was succeeded by Stanley Baldwin, a leading figure in the Unionist revolt against the late Coalition. Baldwin, in many respects a kindly man, loathed Lloyd George to the point of mania. He even defaced photographs of him in his private photograph album. He regarded it as his duty to restore dignity and unity to British politics after the adventures of 1918 to 1922. This meant keeping Lloyd George out of office for ever. There would be no more 'dynamic forces' at the helm if Baldwin could help it. 'Safety first', a policy of passivity, caution and social harmony would be the approach from now on.

The other leading personality in the politics of the 1920s was Ramsay MacDonald, elected leader of the Parliamentary Labour Party in 1922. He was even more hostile towards Lloyd George. For MacDonald had become, almost in spite of himself, the voice of anti-war, even pacifist opposition towards the wartime government, the very symbol of a new era of international harmony. More than most, he had suffered ostracism and persecution during the war and at the 'coupon election' (when he had lost his seat at Leicester). When he

PREVIOUS PAGE
Lloyd George on his farm at Churt in 1935.

OPPOSITE Stanley Baldwin, Conservative prime minister, whose loathing of Lloyd George led him even to deface photographs of him in his private photograph album.

re-emerged from the wilderness and soon became the first Labour prime minister in January 1924, he kept his distance from the Liberals and rejected all proposals for a union of the left. Lloyd George, for his part, had no high opinion of the vain, unstable MacDonald. 'Just a fussy Baldwin, nothing more,' he wrote to his daughter Megan in 1924. The first two Labour governments of 1924 and 1929 to 1931, when in each case Labour was dependent on Liberal support in the House of Commons, saw relations between Lloyd George and MacDonald deteriorate still further. A union of the anti-Conservative forces became more and more improbable. In any case, MacDonald set his face sternly against it. With men such as Baldwin and

Ramsay MacDonald, leader of the Labour Party, whose hostility towards Lloyd George was matched by Lloyd George's own opinion of MacDonald as 'just a fussy Baldwin, nothing more'.

MacDonald dominating politics until the mid-1930s, there was scant prospect of Lloyd George making any real comeback.

With the prospect of union with either of the two main parties highly remote, Lloyd George still floated from time to time his favourite idea of a 'Centre Party'. This scheme had some currency about 1928 to 1929, when he was thought to be seeking the assistance perhaps of press lords like Rothermere and Beaverbrook, perhaps of political mavericks like the Chancellor of the Exchequer, Churchill, perhaps of old aides like Philip Kerr. But nothing ever came of these dreams: 'fusion' had been finally buried in 1920. Not until industrial tycoons in the late 1960s broached the idea of 'Great Britain Limited', a corporate state run on supra-party lines, did anything resembling it re-emerge, and by that time there were no Lloyd Georges left in political life.

In these circumstances, then, Lloyd George had no alternative but to seek reunion with Asquith and to find shelter within the old, discredited Liberal Party he had done so much to undermine. His first moves during Bonar Law's premiership were rebuffed by the Asquithians. After all, many of the Coalition Liberal leaders, headed by Churchill, were moving rapidly to the right. Even so, younger Independent Liberals, such as those in the Liberal summer school, knew that without Lloyd George they lacked ideas and inspiration. If they could not win with Lloyd George, neither perhaps could they win without him. 'When Lloyd George returned to the Liberal Party, ideas returned to it,' wrote Charles Masterman, himself now in the twilight of his career. And so it was that at the end of 1923 Asquithian and Lloyd Georgian Liberals staged an elaborate reunion. The occasion for it was Baldwin's declaration at Plymouth in October 1923 in favour of protection of the home market – the first major challenge to free trade since Joseph Chamberlain's tariff reform campaign in 1903. The motive for Baldwin's dramatic declaration at Plymouth has produced much discussion. It seems most likely that it was inspired by fear of Lloyd George. The ex-premier was engaged on a highly successful speaking tour in the United States at the time, partly to raise money. There were widespread fears that he might return with a new programme, perhaps including imperial preference, and then create a new political combination of Liberals and the former Coalitionist Tories, headed by Austen Chamberlain, who stood aloof from Baldwin's government. In fact, Baldwin's gamble proved to be a grave miscalculation. His attack on free trade threatened the ark of the Liberal covenant. Lloyd George and Asquith promptly united their forces, with declarations of fraternal loyalty, and fought on a joint manifesto. The general election of December 1923 saw the Liberals fight a vigorous campaign (more cast in terms of nineteenth-century economics than of twentieth-century politics). The tally of Liberal seats was raised to 157, with many unexpected victories in cathedral cities and seaside resorts. But a more impressive portent was the rise of the Labour Party which captured 191 seats, and shortly assumed government with Liberal support.

Once Labour was in power, the further decline of the Liberals was inexorable. The first Labour government of January to October 1924 was an unhappy episode for the Liberals. Basically, they were unable to decide whether they were a left-wing radical party or an anti-socialist combination of the centre. Either way, they were easily outflanked by the other parties. Nor were they clear whether, or on what terms, to maintain MacDonald's government in power. The divisions of the years before 1923 could not easily be obliterated. In June 1923 Lloyd George, walking with H.A.L. Fisher near Churt, saw a moss-covered tree visibly dying. 'Like the Liberal Party,' was Lloyd George's gloomy comment. When the government fell in October, the ensuing general election was marked by a severe Liberal setback: their tally of seats fell by over a hundred to only forty. Even Asquith, still the party leader, was defeated at Paisley. Lloyd George thus presided over a shattered and enfeebled rump. In the fifty years that followed, the Liberals were to remain a party of outsiders, a party of protest. For no one were the long-term consequences more damaging than for Lloyd George.

His political future was to be continually plagued by legacies of his premiership throughout the rest of the decade. In particular, the old festering animosity between Asquithians and Lloyd Georgians, dating from December 1916, could not be permanently subdued. Although relations between the two leaders were cordial enough for a time – even Mrs Asquith temporarily sacrificed her venomous attacks on Lloyd George in the cause of party unity – there was fatal division over the general strike in May 1926. Asquith, now a peer, was inclined to support Baldwin's government and to see the general strike as basically an issue of law and order. The correct constitutional position, he believed, was to uphold the government's right to govern. Lloyd George, however, was far more critical of Baldwin's handling of discussions with the miners, and far more

sympathetic to the views of the Trades Union Congress. At a time when Churchill and other ministers were preaching class war, Lloyd George called for calm: he pointed out that the trade unions had never advocated violence and had always urged restraint. Asquith disavowed his views. But it became clear that the bulk of the Liberal Party in the country, especially younger Liberals, sympathised with Lloyd George's more radical outlook. Asquith shortly afterwards resigned as party

Lloyd George speaking at Queen's Hall, London, on a reunited Liberal platform during the 1923 election campaign.

The 1926
General Strike.

Unions almost brought the country to a standstill for nine days from 3 to 12 May 1926 before they were eventually forced to capitulate.

ABOVE A convoy on its way from London's East India Docks to the food depots at Hyde Park.
OPPOSITE ABOVE Workers' demonstration at Crewe.
RIGHT Servicemen, employed as strike-breakers, unloading supplies at Neasden Power Station.
FAR RIGHT Mounted police enforcing order following riots in London's East End.

WORKERS
WORLD
UNITE

ASSURANCE COMPANY
C. MISTLIN DENTIST
Dunn & Co. Hat Makers
Dunn & Co. Hat Makers

leader, and Lloyd George succeeded him. The whole episode merely served to worsen relations between Lloyd George and some Asquithian camp followers such as Simon and Maclean. The Liberal civil war was still very much in being.

Liberal disunity was made far worse by the continuing squalid wrangles over the Lloyd George fund. This had now become more than ever a personal war chest since a body of trustees had been set up under the chairmanship of Lord St David's, one of Lloyd George's remaining Welsh Liberal friends. It became caught up in Lloyd George's purchase and reorganisation of United Newspapers Limited, including the *Daily Chronicle*. The sale of his United Newspapers investment shares in 1928 was believed to have brought the fund at least two and a half million pounds. What had begun as a party chest had been gradually transformed into a trust to be disposed of as Lloyd George saw fit, which made him more vulnerable than ever to political criticism. Since Lloyd George had been a relatively poor man until his premiership, his new affluence was an especially sore point. From early 1924 onwards, wearisome negotiations dragged on between the trustees of the Lloyd George fund and the official Liberal Party organisers to try to reach agreement about the disposal of the fund. From the start, talks went badly. At the 1924 general election, despite much pressure from the whips, Lloyd George made only a modest contribution of fifty thousand pounds towards the Liberals' campaign expenses. In the next three years, talks went on about the terms on which further donations could be handed over, who would administer them, and what guarantees there would be that they would be used for constructive purposes. With immense difficulty, it was agreed that a further three hundred thousand pounds would be handed over to the Liberal central organisation for the 1929 general election, but much bad blood remained. Discussions were not helped by the fact that the Liberal Party organiser at this time was Viscount Gladstone, the son of the former prime minister and the target of some of Lloyd George's most scorching recent attacks.

Lloyd George's standpoint in these talks was clear enough. His private fund was a major bargaining counter. He was loath to see it frittered away by former opponents without adequate guarantees. In particular, he pointed out how wasteful it would be to put money into decaying local constituency parties which, in some cases, could not find candidates. Still, it cannot be disputed that his reputation suffered grievously from the continuing wrangles over the fund. The taint of corruption hung over it. His behaviour seemed erratic, even rapacious, like a cunning Welsh peasant hoarding his cash for a rainy day. The more disagreeable aspects of the years of office after 1918 were kept well in the public eye. It confirmed that that premiership, or the memory of it, was now a liability, best forgotten.

On the other hand, the outlook of that premiership continued to shape his political approach in a much more creative sense. Indeed, it gave new inspiration and life to British politics during the 1920s. In the mid-1920s he began to reassemble those teams of private advisers and aides with which he had governed during the years of power. There were personal links with the wartime years like the Quaker sociologist, Seebohm Rowntree, an expert on urban and rural poverty. But most of them were newer men, not associated with Lloyd George or indeed with political life before. Many of them were economists – Walter Layton, Hubert Henderson and Lionel Robbins were prominent among them. Squads of professors were brought to Churt for weekend conferences. They were dubbed, employing the American usage dating from Theodore Roosevelt's days, the 'brains trust'; as they lent their intelligence to devising new schemes to promote industrial recovery after the post-war slump. The most remarkable new recruit was Maynard Keynes, the Cambridge economist who had left the peace delegation at Paris in 1919 and had so viciously attacked the peace settlement in *The Economic Consequences of the Peace*. He was now temporarily reconciled with Lloyd George and was brought into the 'brains trust' to advance his schemes for massive public works and counter-cyclical spending promoted directly by the central government. A series of documents, in multi-coloured books, dealing with Land, Industry and Power, and finally Unemployment, was published. If they alarmed many older Liberals – *The Land and The Nation* (1925) drove Sir Alfred Mond out of the party for good and led to a furious public altercation with Lloyd George – younger radicals were in raptures of delight.

The most remarkable of all was 'the Orange Book', *We Can Conquer Unemployment*, published in early 1929. This was a far-sighted document which argued, with much factual evidence in support, that thousands of unemployed men could be given work on national enterprises such as road building, housing and electrical services and land drainage. Parts of the scheme were echoes of the Development Commission which Lloyd George himself had set up while Chancellor of the Exchequer in 1909. Keynes and Henderson, meanwhile, published a separate

Lloyd George and Sir Alfred Mond, who eventually left the Liberal Party in 1925 following violent disagreement over Lloyd George's proposals for changes in land tenure.

pamphlet, *Can Lloyd George Do It?*, which showed that, apart from the men directly given employment, many others would benefit from the revival of trade and the increase of purchasing power. The famous 'multiplier' effect of public spending was explained for almost the first time. It was an attractive and compelling scheme – perhaps over-optimistic in its estimates of the immediate impact it would have on the economy – but persuasive and radical. It was a progressive alternative to Tory protection and to socialism. It offered a new impulse of leadership which could break through the stagnation and unemployment with which British industry had been shackled in the post-war years. Under Lloyd George's direction, the beginnings of modern counter-cyclical action by the central government were outlined for the first time. Beyond this, he contemplated a new executive machine, something on the lines of the War Cabinet of 1916. The dream of a new kind of politics to cut through the sterility of the Baldwin years still haunted him.

Basically, Lloyd George still hankered after the presidential style. His premiership of 1916 to 1922 still offered the model for his view of leadership. But that premiership, as has been seen, was also his greatest handicap. Ideas and experts were not enough. He needed also supporters, organisation, a party base – above all, public trust. These were assets which Lloyd George, however fertile in ideas and initiatives, conspicuously lacked. The consequences were fatally revealed in the 1929 general election. Lloyd George dominated that campaign, with his spectacular blueprints to combat depression. He provided a vivid contrast to Baldwin's programme of 'Safety First' and MacDonald's pleas that there should be no monkeying. Labour and the Conservatives vied with each other in their economic orthodoxy. In terms of ideas and vitality, Lloyd George swept the board. But these programmes were being proclaimed by the discredited premier of 1918, whose vehicle was the enfeebled Liberal Party, still tortured by arguments about the Lloyd George fund. This killed any hope Lloyd George ever had of a return to power. The Liberals finished up with only fifty-nine seats: they polled especially badly in the cities, best of all in the more thinly populated parts of the Celtic fringe. Labour, by contrast, won 287 seats, capturing most of the mass working-class vote, and MacDonald became premier a second time. Lloyd George's last serious bid for power had failed totally.

After 1929 he steadily withdrew from front-line activity. The second Labour government was another depressing experience for the Liberals as it was for the country in general. They faced endless problems in maintaining relations with the Labour Party, for example in trying to get Labour to push on such favoured Liberal measures as voting reform. Meanwhile, several right-wing Liberals, headed by Simon and Runciman, drifted over to the Conservatives. When the financial crisis struck in the summer of 1931, and the Labour government resigned on 23 to 24 August, Lloyd George was not a central figure in the manoeuvres that followed. In any case, he was seriously weakened by an operation at the time, and it was Herbert Samuel who represented the Liberals in the discussions that followed. He associated the Liberals with the new so-called 'national government', achieved on the basis of a permanent division of the Labour Party. Lloyd George was full of foreboding – it was hardly the kind of national administration that he envisaged, especially with MacDonald staying on as prime minister. The formation of the government led to yet more divisions within the Liberal Party – indeed, within the Lloyd George family since his son, Gwilym, now member for Pembrokeshire, temporarily took office under MacDonald. At the general election of October 1931, when the government asked vaguely for a 'doctor's mandate', the Liberals divided into three groups. The smallest of them was that headed by Lloyd George. It consisted of just four members – himself, his daughter Megan, his son Gwilym, and his family relative Goronwy Owen, all representing Welsh seats. This was only a small family remnant. Now indeed the Welsh outsider was truly alone.

Still, even in his later sixties and early seventies, the dream of national leadership that had haunted him since December 1916 had not been forgotten. During the years after 1931 he was largely preoccupied with writing his war memoirs, either at Churt, or else abroad at Marrakesh, Montego Bay and elsewhere, fighting with new zest the old battles of 1914. As always Frances Stevenson was his invaluable assistant, the closest person in his life, as she had been for twenty years past. Then in January 1935 Lloyd George rallied himself for a last crusade. He announced the launching of a Council of Action for Peace and Reconstruction. It advocated the old programmes of 1929 – public works, active government intervention in the economy to promote employment, a new style of national executive. Many of his basic political assumptions now re-emerged. He used an array of nonconformist ministers to lend his programme a moral appeal: to the end, he retained his faith in the ability of the nonconformist conscience to sway the nation. He also made wide use of the press. As before, he had much to say about agriculture. The Welsh rural radical in him was far from dormant. He was still convinced that the land question was central to British social and economic recovery, however illusory this appeared to sober economists. Many called it Britain's 'New Deal', adopting the name of Roosevelt's programmes in the United States at the time. But the main inspiration for the Council of Action lay clearly in the wartime policies pursued in Britain after 1915.

The Council of Action for a time captured widespread public attention. 'The Press full of it. The Lobbies also. There is, they say, no other topic of conversation in the House,'

Lloyd George strolling through the grounds of Churt in January 1931 with his daughter Megan, herself now an MP.

The Depression of the 1920s and 30s brought widespread unemployment and suffering. Mass demonstrations were frequent, such as this hunger march to London in 1932 protesting against the hated means test.

Frances Stevenson noted in her diary, with inevitable exaggeration. For a tantalising moment in April and May 1935 it seemed that Lloyd George might even join the National government. Talks began with the Cabinet, in which Lloyd George explained his remedies for unemployment. But it was all a bit unreal. The animosity of Baldwin and MacDonald towards the 'big beast' (or 'goat') was unrelenting and unforgiving. There was never much likelihood of Lloyd George being taken back by the men of 1922. An even more bitter foe was the Chancellor of the Exchequer, Neville Chamberlain, whom Lloyd George had dismissed from the wartime government long ago in 1917. Lloyd George regarded him as a pale reflection of his father. 'Not a bad mayor of Birmingham in a lean year,' was his biting verdict. Despite all the efforts of Thomas Jones as intermediary, on 1 July 1935, Frances Stevenson noted that discussions had been finally broken off. 'They knew in their hearts they were about to knife me. What they did not know was that I too had a dagger in my sheath for them,' was Lloyd George's typically aggressive response. He was referring to the Council of Action, which, in fact, began to lose momentum as the Free Church ministers and others began to back down. Lloyd George's final attempt to remodel British government and re-direct British economic policy had foundered.

At the general election of October 1935, the Independent Liberals, all those outside the ranks of the National government, won a mere twenty-one seats. Lloyd George, obviously rejected by the electorate once and for all, retired to resume the writing of his war memoirs and his defence of the peace treaties. The politics of the past captured his imagination far more readily now than did the conflicts of the present.

There was still, however, one major area in which the memories of his premiership continued to shape his attitude towards current events. As one of the major architects of the peace settlement in 1919, and the only one to survive it, he was naturally much involved in the controversies over international affairs. As the 1930s brought the coming of dictatorship in Germany, Austria, Spain and elsewhere; as collective security broke down with the manifest ineffectiveness of the League of Nations, Lloyd George inevitably took a leading part in public debate. From 1934 he tried to emerge again in his familiar role as the great mediator, perhaps the one man who could reconcile the ambitions of Hitler and Mussolini with the needs of British security. He launched severe criticisms of the foreign policies of the National government. More important, the course of events since 1933 added to a growing disillusionment on his part about the adequacy of western parliamentary democracy ever to deal with the challenge of the dictators. While Britain was enfeebled and undermined by the passive leadership of men like Baldwin and Chamberlain, abroad there were dynamic leaders at the helm. Lloyd George was impressed by Roosevelt's 'New Deal' in the United States after March 1933, however much it differed from his own. Some of Roosevelt's methods and policies – the use of a 'brains trust' of advisers and experts; the use of government intervention to 'prime the pump' of the economy and restore growth; the extension of social welfare; above all, the use of 'broad executive power' by the president – suggested vividly to Lloyd George some of the techniques that could be used by a less inert government in Britain.

Lloyd George's enthusiastic response to Hitler and his policies caused a considerable stir in Britain. Following his famous meeting with Hitler in 1936 (opposite) Lloyd George pronounced him 'the George Washington of Germany'. He was equally impressed by the projects he inspected on his tour there.
BELOW Lloyd George gives the Nazi salute during a visit to a women's labour camp.

Even more was he fascinated by the rise of Hitler. Indeed, many of his contributions to the public debate on foreign policy from 1934 onwards took the form of suggestions that a deal with Hitler was possible and desirable. After all, Lloyd George himself had been an advocate of moderate treatment of Germany over reparations and frontier arrangements since he framed the Fontainebleau memorandum in March 1919. He now urged that concessions could and should be made over the Saar, Danzig, the Polish corridor, and the Rhineland. He demanded

that Hitler's offer of a long-term, non-aggression pact be accepted. At the time of Munich he was still urging an attempt to come to terms with Hitler, while criticising the feeble conduct of negotiations by Chamberlain and Daladier. Even after war broke out in September 1939, he was to propose that the door be left open for a negotiated peace. Hitler was in many ways the political leader who crystallised those gifts which Lloyd George most admired. He had courage, he had charismatic qualities of inspiration and mass leadership, he came from a humble background and claimed to look at political issues free from outmoded class prejudice. He represented himself as 'the unknown soldier of Germany', come to purge Germany's despair and depression after the Weimar Republic had collapsed and the German economy had crashed down in ruins.

Lloyd George had an historic meeting with Hitler at his mountain villa at Berchtesgaden in Bavaria in September 1936. Thomas Jones, the former assistant secretary to the Cabinet and a notable 'appeaser' who accompanied him, has left us a vivid record of this meeting. Face to face were the statesman who had dominated the First World War, leonine with flowing white hair, still a bewitching figure, and the restless, magnetic personality of Hitler. The Bavarian Alps provided a back-cloth of Wagnerian splendour. The two leaders got on exceptionally well. Hitler handed Lloyd George a signed photograph of himself, addressed 'to the man who won the war'. Lloyd George responded by calling Hitler 'the greatest living German', who had given his people a new hope and inspiration after years of despair. In their talks, the two leaders ranged widely over international affairs as they had unfolded since 1919. They did not agree on all issues – Lloyd George made plain his hostility to Franco's rebellion against the Republican régime in Spain, for instance. But they were united in demanding a new reconciliation between Britain and Germany, partly to combat the threat of bolshevism.

Lloyd George was also taken on a tour of German public works projects, road building, land reclamation and similar enterprises, all of which impressed him mightily. On returning to Britain, he sang the praises of Hitler in an uncritical and euphoric manner. In the *Daily Express*, despite the efforts of his colleagues to tone down his superlatives, he was lyrical in his enthusiasm for Hitler. 'He is a born leader of men. A magnetic, dynamic personality with a single-minded purpose, a resolute will and a dauntless heart. . . . He is the George Washington of Germany.' Lloyd George added for good measure: 'The

Anthony Eden leaving the Foreign Office on his resignation over the Austrian crisis in 1938.

Germans have definitely made up their minds never to quarrel with us again.'

Despite this wild eulogy, which added to the suspicions widely entertained about the ageing statesman's judgement, it would be wrong to see him as just an uncritical advocate of appeasement of Germany. On the contrary, more than any other figure in British public life, he had unrivalled knowledge of the aggressive aspects of German nationalism, and its urge to acquire territory in the east. He urged, therefore, simultaneously with efforts to reach diplomatic agreement with Germany, a steady build-up of British armed strength, especially the air force, so that Britain could confront the dictators from a position of strength. He made a devastating attack on Baldwin in June 1936 for his 'cowardly surrender' in failing to check Italian aggression in Abyssinia (although it must be said that Lloyd George had previously encouraged Grandi, the Italian foreign minister, to acquire territory in the area). He denounced the craven humiliation of the Hoare–Laval pact. He demanded naval support by Britain for the Republicans during the civil war in Spain and condemned as a farce the 'non-intervention' preached by Eden, the foreign secretary in 1936. Lloyd George was also a fierce critic of the Munich settlement in September 1938. It was, he said, totally one-sided, an imposed solution forced on Czechoslovakia, not at all the kind of reciprocal agreement with Hitler that he had demanded. One especially persistent theme of his in these years was the demand for an alliance with the Soviet Union, another of his objectives in foreign affairs since he had wound up the allied invasion of Soviet Russia in 1920. He struck up an unlikely friendship with Maisky, the Russian ambassador in London, who regarded Lloyd George as a leading champion of Anglo-Russian friendship. Maisky was to send the old man a warm personal letter to commemorate his eightieth birthday in 1943. Lloyd George, with Maisky's support, fiercely and brilliantly attacked the guarantee to Poland given by Chamberlain in March 1939. It would, Lloyd George correctly argued, be pointless without an alliance with the Soviet Union. His fears were borne out in September 1939 when the guarantee to Poland, an empty moral gesture which neither Britain nor France could do anything to implement, led directly to the nation being swept into another world war.

Lloyd George had, naturally, been a somewhat withdrawn figure in these later years. The general public had the impression now of an elder statesman quietly cultivating his apples and raspberries at Churt. His estate there grew to seven hundred and fifty acres. His main preoccupation for much of the time was the writing of his memoirs of the First World War and the peace treaties. He was unsparing in fighting again the old battles against Haig and Robertson. While Frances Stevenson slaved away as a research assistant, the military correspondent, Basil Liddell Hart, read through and revised the accounts of the military aspect of the war. The *War Memoirs* appeared in six volumes between 1933 and 1936; *The Truth about the Peace Treaties* came out in two volumes in 1938. Despite their partisan quality and the monotonous infallibility which the author claimed for himself, they were, deservedly, a considerable commercial success.

He was still, though, a significant figure in current affairs. Many bright young men in politics, men like Robert Boothby, Brendan Bracken and Dingle Foot, made the pilgrimage down to Churt. Quite apart from basking in Lloyd George's unequalled charm of conversation, they still entertained the hope that the old giant would emerge from the wings, that he could be persuaded to assume leadership of the nation in a crisis even graver than that of 1916. Brendan Bracken, speaking for younger Tory opinion, put pressure on Lloyd George in this sense in 1935. Many in the press and in parliament wrote hopefully of a Lloyd George comeback, despite the manifest signs of failing physical energies on the part of a man who was seventy-six when the Second World War broke out. But it was becoming apparent that elder statesmen, like heavyweight boxing champions, seldom returned.

Even after September 1939, though, Lloyd George was still a major influence on the political scene. He was amongst those involved in advocating a possible negotiated peace during the so-called 'phoney war' that continued until April 1940. On the other hand, he was persuaded to lend his authority to the growing criticism heard on both sides of the House of the leadership of Neville Chamberlain. This reached an acute pitch after the débâcle of the expedition to Norway in April 1940 and the subsequent German invasion of the Low Countries. With the aid of his daughter Megan, he was persuaded to take part in the famous debate in the Commons on 7 to 8 May 1940 in which Chamberlain was finally overthrown. Many critics made weighty attacks on the prime minister, but it was Lloyd George's appeal for the premier's supreme sacrifice of the seals of office that electrified the House. When the government's majority was seen to have fallen from over two hundred to a mere eighty, Chamberlain had to resign, Churchill succeeding him.

Would Churchill, a long-standing associate, now bring Lloyd George into the government? Many in the press hoped that he might. J.L.Garvin, the editor of *The Observer* and formerly a staunch supporter of the 1918 to 1922 coalition, urged that Lloyd George be brought in to administer the nation's food supplies. Lloyd George, Garvin wrote, might be good for only six hours a day – 'but they would be six hours of pure radium'. In the event, discussions between the war leader of 1916 and that of 1940 were half-hearted on each side. Churchill suspected Lloyd George of having defeatist tendencies. His admiration for Hitler was still fresh in the memory. Perhaps the Welsh wizard would finish up as a British Pétain? Lloyd George, Churchill thought, no longer had 'the root of the matter' within him. By contrast, Lloyd George was well aware of his advancing years; perhaps he felt also that it wasn't his war. There were vague discussions in June and July about Lloyd George entering the War Cabinet, but no firm proposals resulted. In November, when Lord Lothian (the old friend, Philip Kerr) died, Lloyd George was, amazingly enough, offered the succession as British ambassador in Washington. After a few days' deliberation, he turned it

Dame Margaret Lloyd George who died at Criccieth in 1941.

down. He and Churchill were never to be in close contact again.

The last years were somewhat pathetic. Although relations with Dame Margaret had been distant for many years they had celebrated their golden wedding together in January 1938. In 1941 she died unexpectedly, and Lloyd George's efforts to reach her bedside before she died were frustrated by heavy snowfalls in the Welsh mountains. Two years later, he married Frances Stevenson. Relations with other members of the family, especially Megan, regarded as his political heir and now member for Anglesey, became more and more tense. Lloyd George still emerged in political debate occasionally. He was a pessimistic critic of the course of the war. He viewed allied successes from El Alamein onwards without much enthusiasm or hope. He was physically afraid of the German air raids. The wartime years at his home were enlivened by public hearings of 'Lord Haw Haw's' radio broadcasts, for which Lloyd George showed a remarkable relish.

By the end of 1944 the old man, now over eighty-one years of

Lloyd George on his eightieth birthday with his two daughters Olwen (left) and Megan.

age, was obviously breaking up. He decided, therefore, on a last visit to Wales. He had always kept up close contact with his native land. His annual Thursday presidency at the national *eisteddfod* was still a treasured event. He continued to visit the Welsh Baptist chapel at Castle Street, London, as he had done since becoming an MP in 1890. He made his customary annual speech there on 'Flower Sunday'. He now came home to Wales for the last time. While there, it was announced, on 1 January 1945, to the general surprise, that the Great Commoner of Wales had become Earl Lloyd-George of Dwyfor. One factor in this decision was that his seat of Caernarvon Boroughs, which he had held for fifty-four years, was now very vulnerable. In fact, in the 1945 general election it was to be won by a Conservative. Still, the spectacle of Lloyd George, of all people, going to the House of Lords, which he had done so much to discredit in the past, undermined his reputation amongst many Welsh Liberals. It weakened further his tarnished reputation as a man of the left. He died at the age of eighty-two, on 26 March 1945, in the

OPPOSITE Frances Stevenson and Lloyd George shortly after their marriage in 1943.

rival presences of his daughter Megan, and his second wife Frances. After a simple burial service his body was laid to rest in a wood beside the river Dwyfor where he had spent so much of his boyhood. A great boulder now marks his grave. There is no inscription.

The Lloyd George tradition was carried on in political life for a further quarter of a century. His son Gwilym, member for Pembrokeshire, joined the Conservatives and served (as Home Secretary, among other offices) under Churchill and Eden in the 1950s. Megan, by contrast, moved left and joined the Labour Party; she was always the radical of the family. She was elected for Carmarthen in 1957 and held the seat until her death in 1966. Her constituency was captured after her death by a Welsh Nationalist, Gwynfor Evans. Perhaps this outcome was not an inappropriate comment on Lloyd George's political memory. His other daughter, Lady Olwen, remained aloof from politics. A final living link with the old traditions, one still bitterly divided from the Lloyd George family, was Frances, the Countess, who continued to lead an active career. Her diaries, published in 1971 under the editorship of A.J.P.Taylor, helped towards an increasingly favourable assessment of her late husband's personality and political objectives. They showed Lloyd George as a vulnerable human being, capable of sympathy and affection. Only with the death of the Countess in December 1972 could it be said that the links that bound David Lloyd George to British public life had been finally and irrevocably snapped.

Historians in recent years have rightly pointed out that the later phase of Lloyd George's career from 1922 to 1945 was far from being the long diminuendo that was once alleged. He was without doubt a major political figure throughout the inter-war period. A political comeback was thought to be distinctly possible at least until 1929, maybe even until 1940. He played a major role in adding new vitality to British public life throughout this period. His schemes for promoting economic recovery in the later 1920s were the only major radical proposals of the time; some of them were to become part of the conventional economic wisdom after 1945. Apart perhaps from Sir Oswald Mosley, Lloyd George was the only political leader offering constructive and forward-looking remedies for the damage wrought to the British economy by the Great War – and his ideas were compatible with a democratic system, as Mosley's, distorted as they were by racialism, were not. In the 1930s, Lloyd George was a formidable critic of British foreign policy,

particularly of the passive form which appeasement took under Baldwin and Chamberlain. He urged a flexible, many-sided policy in which the build-up of military, naval and air power should coincide with a positive effort to negotiate away the real grievances under which Germany was said to be labouring. There were many at the time who would echo the views frequently put forward later on by Lord Boothby, that Lloyd George's relegation to the sidelines in the inter-war period was a national tragedy, one in which his gifts of leadership were wantonly thrown away. Churchill, of course, was also in the shadows during the 1930s until his moment came in 1939. But in the sphere of domestic reform, as well as of international reconciliation, Lloyd George had unique creative qualities to offer. They were spurned.

At the same time, it is not surprising that his later period in politics was so unsatisfying and ineffective. The legacy of 1918 lingered on. From being at one time his greatest asset, his record as prime minister had become his major handicap in a world in which the British sought the comfort of the conventional politics of pre-1914 rather than unpredictable adventures. In view of Lloyd George's record, it was hard to take seriously his pledges of pious devotion to the Liberal Party, especially when the Lloyd George fund testified to his abiding distrust of his Liberal colleagues. Although he continued to put forward policies under the Liberal banner, although he was clearly to be distinguished from both the Labour and Tory positions, his Liberalism was not obviously associated with the Liberal Party either. He was still the outsider, protected by his private entourage at Churt. Even while he led the Liberal Party, there were still indications that he hankered after some new political formation on the lines of his abortive Centre Party in 1920, and this merely added to the distrust that surrounded him. His enthusiasm for foreign dictators also aroused suspicion. When he could voice his admiration for Hitler and Mussolini in so unbridled a manner, was there perhaps a Fascist streak even in so rooted a democrat as Lloyd George? At the very least, he gave the constant impression of seeking to import alien traditions into the British political system. Perhaps in the 1970s the British, propelled against their will into the Common Market, are somewhat less insular, less prone to take a Gilbert-and Sullivan view of borrowing from other nations. In the 1920s and 1930s clearly they were not. It is, then, a basic criticism of Lloyd George's judgement of events that he overestimated his countrymen's willingness to experiment, and their

OPPOSITE Lloyd George's coffin being carried on a farm cart to the funeral service.

unwillingness to forgive and forget. As a result, he was viewed more and more as an exotic growth, not really relevant to the running of day-to-day affairs. By 1939, he was regarded, in the words of a not unsympathetic Welsh observer, as 'the sarcophagus of British radicalism', a survivor from a dead era who had somehow lingered on into the contemporary world. To the younger generation, especially, Lloyd George seemed to have little to offer now. The passing of Lloyd George, while a major landmark to the historian and to private groups of admirers and disciples, went largely unnoticed by most contemporaries. Once the very symbol of radical experiment, he had become a part of the world we have lost.

7

LLOYD GEORGE IN PERSPECTIVE

IN THE TWENTY-NINE YEARS that have passed since Lloyd George's death, he has continued to stir up furious argument amongst historians and biographers. Many of the latter – for instance Thomas Jones, whose biography appeared in 1951 – were generally sympathetic, even if their enthusiasm was somewhat guarded. But the dominant tendency in the interpretations of Lloyd George's career until the mid-1960s was overwhelmingly critical. Writers of varying political persuasions unsparingly heaped condemnation on his private and public life. Books written by those close to the former prime minister made their own special contribution to this process. A.J. Sylvester's *The Real Lloyd George* (1947), a volume written by his personal secretary, had a disagreeable revelatory tone. It depicted Lloyd George as essentially a peevish, autocratic old man. The biography by the second Earl in 1960 laid the main emphasis on his father's cruelty to his mother, and on his physical lust. The very name of Lloyd George, it seemed, had become synonymous with private and public decadence. When in 1963 the Macmillan government was undermined by sexual scandals, critics commented that it was all reminiscent of the atmosphere of decay of Lloyd George's premiership. (Significantly, the Lambton–Jellicoe scandals of 1973 brought no such comparison.) When Harold Wilson in the later 1960s was assailed for prime ministerial domination, allied to close-quarters intrigue, Lloyd George was again the parallel that commonly sprang to mind. He seemed to have become a kind of universal pariah, pilloried for the various ills under which twentieth-century Britain laboured.

Only in the years since 1966, partly through the opening up of new sources in the Beaverbrook Library and the National Library of Wales, has Lloyd George become largely rehabilitated in public esteem. He is a scapegoat no longer. When the play *Lloyd George Knew my Father* appeared at the Savoy Theatre in London in the early 1970s, the title was a joke, not a serious political comment. Almost every major work of scholarship written in the past six or seven years on recent British political history has taken a far more balanced view of him than seemed likely at the time of his death. At last he may be turning into a credible historical figure, capable of being understood, even admired.

To an astonishing degree, the controversy about him has taken the form of a continuing debate about his private life. The sexual proclivities of no other prime minister have aroused quite the same kind of obsessive inquiry. Of course, prime

PREVIOUS PAGE Lloyd George as President of the Board of Trade in 1906.

ministers galore before Lloyd George had mistresses – Wellington, Canning, Palmerston, Disraeli are instances that come readily to mind. So too did many of Lloyd George's political contemporaries – Curzon, F.E. Smith, and notably Asquith (with his passionate affair with the youthful Lady Venetia Stanley) are conspicuous examples here. Even so, the belief still persists that Lloyd George was somehow in a unique category as a womanizer on the grand scale, pursuing women almost indiscriminately from society hostesses to office typists. In this vein, Lord Annan in 1972 declared that Lloyd George 'had no principles, no scruples and no heart'. The volume that added most credence to these charges was that of the second Earl Lloyd George which, as has been seen, depicted his father as an oversexed libertine: his mother, by contrast, was portrayed as the very symbol of wronged womanhood. Even John Grigg's sympathetic recent study of Lloyd George, which is exceptionally fair in treating most aspects of his subject's private life, still finds it possible to describe him as a 'male philanderer' and to devote thirty pages to necessarily inconclusive discussion of his relations with Mrs Edwards (of the paternity case) and with Mrs Timothy Davies.

Now that new evidence, either not released before or else wilfully ignored by earlier historians, is available, these charges can be reduced to their proper perspective. Now that we have in print the diary of his second wife, and his correspondence with Dame Margaret, Lloyd George's private morality can be viewed in historical terms. It is quite obvious that the image of an unbridled libertine is a total myth: Lloyd George was above all the complete professional politician dedicated to public objectives, not to private lust. The second Earl's book is unreliable, based to some considerable degree on gossip. There is ample evidence, certainly, that Lloyd George was readily attracted to pretty women, as were many other members of parliament, then and later. But it is clear also that he was a faithful, and in some ways devoted, husband of Margaret Owen for at least the first twenty years of their married life. The one personal crisis they underwent, the Edwards' divorce case in 1897, was resolved without Lloyd George even having to enter the witness-box. The evidence suggests that it was Mrs Edwards, coquettish, bored with the life of a country doctor's wife, who pursued Lloyd George rather than the other way around. His marriage survived largely unimpaired.

Lloyd George's relations with other women were a topic of teasing humour between him and Margaret in their early

correspondence, but seldom caused difficulty. What gradually drove them apart was not women but Wales – Margaret's dogged refusal to join her husband in London when his parliamentary career inevitably drew him away from Criccieth. Somehow she had persuaded herself along the way that she had married Lloyd George simply as a country attorney, and had never expected him to go into politics. It was a total delusion. As a result of her unwillingness to leave Wales to join her husband, even at Christmas time or on summer holidays, the private letters between Lloyd George and his wife between 1890 and 1902 are full of his despairing pleas to her to come to keep him company. In London, he was hungry, lonely, even frightened. He had to breakfast alone on 'cold coffee, grapenuts, eternal ham'. 'I have scores of times come home in the dead of night to a cold, dark and comfortless flat without a soul to greet me,' he added. 'I am not the nature either physically or morally that I ought to have been left like this. . . . You have been a good mother. You have not – and I say this now not in anger – not always been a good wife.' Her failure to respond, apart from intermittent visits, led him in the end to seek solace elsewhere. Part of the attraction of Mrs Timothy Davies was that she kept a comfortable house and could give Lloyd George decent meals. Yet he retained his meed of affection for his first wife, despite their growing estrangement. In some sense, he needed her to the end, her placid guidance, her calmness, her strength of character, her reassuring contacts with the world of Welsh village democracy he knew and loved.

OPPOSITE Lloyd George with his wife Margaret and their daughter Olwen.

Frances Stevenson, by contrast, offered him something else – a sophisticated assurance in the world of high politics, the world of manipulation and manoeuvre in London. She also offered him a more complete emotional relationship: her diary is a moving insight into the storms that beset Lloyd George during the years of power and his need for a peaceful refuge with her in Churt or elsewhere. Frances Stevenson experienced a warm, tender side of Lloyd George which few suspected. When she was ill in early 1915, at a period of acute political crisis, Lloyd George was always at hand to nurse her back to health. 'I do not think I can every repay him for his goodness to me,' she wrote (11 March 1915).

> He has been husband, lover and mother to me. I never knew a man could be so womanly & tender. He has watched and waited on me devotedly until I cursed myself for being so ill and causing him all this worry. . . . If those who idolise him as a public man could know the full greatness of his heart, how much more their idol would he be! And

Frances Stevenson walking through Paris with Megan during the peace conferences which she was attending as Lloyd George's private secretary.

through it all he has been immersed in great decisions appertaining to this great crisis. . . .

She also noted his affection for his family, for dear old Uncle Lloyd, and for his children. Lloyd George, she wrote (30 November 1914) 'is a terrible man for worrying where anyone he is fond of is concerned. He is much too sensitive for a man, much too tender-hearted.' In these moments, Frances Stevenson was far closer to Lloyd George than was any other human being. On the other hand, the rural Wales of his youth, the values of which remained so important to him, she never really understood. After all it was associated with a hostile world, particularly with the Lloyd George family who, not surprisingly, treated her like an outcast. Like her, they were good haters.

The truth about Lloyd George's private life appears to be much less sensational than recent scandalous accounts have hinted. There was no lustful 'mask of Merlin'. Lloyd George's abiding affections were confined to two women, and only two.

Each of them responded to a different quality in his make-up, and in his scale of values. Dame Margaret kept him close to the old democratic roots; Frances provided solace at the centre of politics. One reminded him of the foothills; the other protected him at the summit. However unorthodox it may appear to the severer kind of moralist, Lloyd George needed the two women in his life and displayed loyalty and affection towards them both. As Professor John Vincent has cogently written, 'Lloyd George's best-kept secret is out – respectability'.

Other charges also made about his character will also have to be modified. It has often been alleged that he was incapable of friendship; that he was ruthless and unforgiving in sacrificing associates. 'He had no friends and did not deserve any,' A.J.P. Taylor once wrote. F.S. Oliver had written of Lloyd George years before, 'He does not understand what friendship means.' In fact, Lloyd George was a man with profound human qualities. He was, it is true, a belligerent person, prepared to smash down all obstacles that lay in his path. He could be unsparing if friendship got in the way of the fulfilment of higher political objectives. Masterman, for instance, was cast aside when he mishandled an electoral dispute in a Welsh constituency in 1914. Addison had to go when he totally bungled the financing of the housing programme in 1921. Edwin Montagu, David Davies, Sir Alfred Mond, Maynard Keynes, all close associates at one time, discovered how implacable and crushing Lloyd George's wrath could be. Hayes Fisher, who mishandled the electoral register in 1918 was dealt with ferociously. 'I don't care whether you drown him in a butt of Malmsey; he must be a dead chicken by tonight,' Lloyd George commanded imperiously. And he was.

Yet here was also a man with a rare gift for human communication and sympathy, when he chose to show it. He had the hypnotic magic which, it was said, 'could charm a bird off a bough'. He was a man with immense charm for women, a man devoted to children, tender towards the old and above all to Uncle Lloyd. Throughout his career, he forged close friendships with such different figures as the respectable Welsh Liberal, Herbert Lewis; the Ulster-Canadian Unionist, Bonar Law; the Christian socialist, Charles Masterman; an editor like C.P.Scott; a don like H.A.L.Fisher; a general like Sir Henry Wilson; even with the Russian ambassador, Ivan Maisky. These friendships were, it is true, essentially political; but Lloyd George is hardly unique amongst prime ministers in allowing professional considerations to determine his scale of values. At the same time, he was free from enduring prejudices, and therefore was without grudges. Personal pique never prevented his trying to build bridges towards opponents, as he did towards Asquith after 1922. In many ways, indeed, he seems a much warmer, more human personality, more attuned to human intimacy than were his leading contemporaries – for instance, Grey, Asquith, Haldane and Oxford-bred patricians of this kind. Lloyd George gave of himself more freely than did they; consequently he was the more vulnerable when friendships broke down. In personal terms, he was essentially the great democrat, perhaps most able to relax in the company of self-made businessmen and press lords, but readily approachable to Welsh working men whom he met at Castle Street chapel or in his constituency, as the present writer's family can

Lloyd George with his daughter Megan following a presentation ceremony at Seven Sisters in 1911.

testify. The toughness, strength of nerve and even ruthlessness, inseparable from the career of a major statesman, did not render him the less capable of human fellowship. Perhaps the best testimony of all to this is his friendship with Churchill, despite all the vicissitudes that beset their careers. One index of Churchill's greatness of spirit was his capacity to recognise greatness in the older man, even his willingness to settle happily for a 'master-servant' relationship. Churchill's tribute to Lloyd George in the House of Commons at the time of his death conveys movingly the essential flavour of their long friendship which lasted, with periods of distrust and jealousy on either side, almost to the end.

Other charges made about Lloyd George's private life also need to be looked at more closely. Over money matters, he was less culpable than has sometimes been alleged. The Patagonian gold-mining venture in the 1890s dealt unsparingly with many poor, gullible shareholders, and Lloyd George was partly to blame. But he remained for many years a comparatively poor man, largely dependent on his private solicitor's practice with incidental journalism for income. There was some suggestion during his period at the Board of Trade in 1907 that he might be granted an allowance from central party funds. Lloyd George rejected the idea: he had no wish to become the party's 'doormat'. The Marconi case of 1912 was a tribute to foolishness rather than to dishonesty. He rushed into the purchase of shares without giving the matter much attention, and in fact lost money on the deal. He remained amongst the least well-off members of the government, with a frugal, almost drab style of life. Even after his becoming prime minister in 1916, his personal finances did not greatly improve: the Lloyd George fund was from the outset devoted solely to political organization. After he left office in 1922, however, it is certainly true that he became far wealthier, with a large estate at Churt, an entourage of private secretaries, and spectacular holidays in such places as Montego Bay as symbols of his new affluence. The main keys to this were an ex-premier's pension of two thousand pounds a year, an annuity from Andrew Carnegie of the same amount, together with the swelling flow of royalties from his memoirs and other writings. He earned between three and five hundred pounds a week from the American press, and three hundred thousand pounds from the sales of his war memoirs. For, of course, an ex-prime minister was a valuable commercial property. Whether or not this later affluence is disreputable is open to many interpretations. Like other public men, in the 1970s no less than in the 1920s, Lloyd George left public life notably wealthier than when he entered it. In recent years, Harold Wilson and Edward Heath have pursued the same path of affluence. This is, without doubt, one of the many unpleasant, unacceptable aspects of capitalism, though it is notable that Labour politicians seem no more squeamish than Tory ones in making use of it. He was unusual mainly in the relative humbleness of his origins. He was not a corrupt man: by the test of most recent American presidents he was the very model of financial rectitude. He had no interest in building up a personal fortune. He turned down offers of city directorships. His concern was with politics to the end. The truth is rather that he was a man with great gifts, with great objectives to promote, and these needed funds. Ambition, not avarice, drove him on. Public life, not personal peculation, led him into the shadier by-ways of financial unorthodoxy. This was essential to his career; and it helped towards his ruin.

To the general public, from Boer War days onwards, Lloyd George was a great mass leader with rare gifts of inspiration. In the House of Commons, he was usually a commanding, perhaps sometimes over-rhetorical speaker. It was his dominance in debate that enabled his government to survive the sacking of Robertson and the Maurice affair in 1918. His addresses on foreign policy in the 1930s showed that the old authority was still present in full. On the public platform he had a unique genius for inspirational oratory. He showed how the pulpit and the music hall could mould the mass communicator. His speeches were invariably painstakingly prepared, studded with striking poetic phrases, and delivered in a light Welsh voice with a beguiling melodic lilt. He could be fired by physical contact with an audience, and play on their emotions and fears with sensitivity and subtlety. He was the ideal orator for the pre-microphone age. The use of radio was a mystery which he was still exploring at the time of his death. Kingsley Martin, the editor of the *New Statesman*, and Lloyd George's daughter, Megan, tried with scant success to get him to address the unseen radio audience with the same spontaneity as he did live crowds. 'We spent hours and days and weeks on him and – NOTHING!', Martin recorded. On television, with his mischievous humour and quickness of wit, his penetrating blue eyes and flowing white mane, Lloyd George would surely have been a superb performer, a match for any interviewer. His speeches do not often read well now. Some of his rural imagery and biblical phraseology appear somewhat trite to readers in the later

twentieth century, weaned on the clipped, unemotional speaking styles of the post-Churchill years. Even so, a radical declamation like the Newcastle speech in October 1910 still seems as challenging and inspiring as when it was delivered. The soaring language, the caustic humour, the visionary peroration are as appealing now as at the time of delivery. Above all, there is a warmth and human sympathy about Lloyd George's best speeches which lend them a timeless quality. They have a dimension which those of Aneurin Bevan, for instance, filled

Lloyd George on his sixty-fourth birthday with his wife Margaret and daughter Megan in the study at Churt.

Lloyd George was a superb orator capable of evoking an intense response from his audience. This address was in commemoration of his old friend Sir Henry Jones, the philosopher. Thomas Jones is seated beside Lloyd George.

with clipped ironies and verbal paradoxes, conspicuously lack. Unlike Bevan, Lloyd George could respond to a wide range of moods and occasions. He could capture the nationalist yearnings of his fellow Welshmen, or the social anxieties of the British mass democracy, or the sense of universal tragedy of a world locked in war. He could, in his greatest speeches, soar beyond his Welsh origins, while never losing touch with the emotions and values of the world in which he was reared. Like Eric Hoffer's True Believer, like F.D.Roosevelt or Gandhi, he 'could harness men's hopes and fears in a holy cause'. This gives his speeches a universal appeal unique among British political leaders since Gladstone's day.

As a writer, his achievements were more uneven. His early ventures in journalism seem pedestrian enough now. Even so, his war memoirs and his studies of the peace treaties, partisan and often unfair though they undoubtedly are, presented an immense mass of invaluable first-hand source material in a forceful and stirring manner. Some of the thumb-nail sketches – of Grey or of Kitchener for instance – are especially memorable. Kitchener is compared with a great lighthouse, which 'radiated momentary gleams of revealing light far out into the surrounding gloom and then suddenly relapsed into complete darkness'. Indeed, Lloyd George's memoirs, as source material and as literature, have stood the test of time far more successfully than have many such essays in self-justification, better than Churchill's writings on the 1914–18 war, and perhaps on the 1939–45 war as well. As a private correspondent, Lloyd George was erratic. He always preferred verbal contact to letter-writing, and comparatively few letters from him survive. Still, his letters to his family reveal at times that same command of language, that same vivid imagery so often seen in his speeches. There is always this proviso: Lloyd George's letters are alive if he is writing about politics. If he turns to deal with domestic affairs, his style becomes flat and banal. In letters as in life, he was the most political of men. Indeed, life generally held little charm for him away from politics. Apart from a few casual relaxations like reading wild-west thrillers or a round of golf, his recreations were set in a political mould. His interest in such historical figures as Napoleon or Lincoln was dictated by their relevance, if any, to contemporary affairs. As his speeches, memoirs and private letters show, remove Lloyd George from politics and the magic disappears. He is egotistical, stilted in expression, almost at times a bore.

His political career, as has been seen, is now increasingly

being subjected to searching revision. More and more, the criticisms hurled at him seem hard to sustain. Above all, it is difficult to see in him just the 'rootless opportunist', 'vampire and medium in one' portrayed by Keynes and others. In methods, certainly, he was endlessly flexible, often deliberately indirect. But opportunism of method was always linked to general consistency of objectives. Indeed, it could be argued that his career was determined by long-term objectives to a degree unusual among British politicians. He was steadfast in his sympathy for the national claims of Wales. He was consistent in his concern for social reform, at least from the time of the visit to Germany in 1908. He was consistent in his belief that Britain ought to be made a more democratic and egalitarian society. He was consistent in his view that British imperial and foreign policy should be linked to the search for international harmony. The architect of victory in 1918, he was essentially a conciliator, a man of peace. His objectives, then, were consistent and progressive. We who have seen the wholesale reversal of the Labour Party's programmes between 1964 and 1970 and then the equally rapid abandonment of the Conservatives' objectives after 1970 can hardly take too seriously the charge that Lloyd George was uniquely opportunist. To a remarkable degree he was a man of principle who took the high road in politics.

His erratic qualities lay rather in the means by which he sought to gain these objectives. Throughout his career he had an intermittent but powerful yearning for a supreme national government, backed by a pliant parliament, press and public opinion. He was never the servant of party, even as a Welsh radical in the 1890s. He deeply admired Theodore Roosevelt's New Nationalism in 1912, with its attempt to deal with American economic problems on a scientific supra-party basis. Ironically enough, he attacked Roosevelt for breaking away to form his own 'Bull Moose' party. 'He should never have quarrelled with the machine' commented Lloyd George: he might have heeded this warning himself in the 'coupon election' of 1918, the root of his own downfall. But the fatal lure of a new 'national' politics had ensnared him by then.

On the other hand, he was certainly capable of party loyalty. It is quite wrong to allege that he was intriguing against Asquith's leadership at any time between 1908 and 1915. It was rather the war, with the new political fluidity it created, that drove a wedge between the two great Liberal leaders which had never existed before. Lloyd George saw how the war had produced a new kind of politics, with party in abeyance. He failed to see how the wartime truce could only be a temporary affair, one which could not long endure the alignments of peace. Hence the abortive search for a 'Centre Party' after 1918. In fact, he had no political home left save the old Liberal Party which he had himself done so much to demoralize. When Lloyd George rejoined the Liberals, he brought with him much of the New Liberalism of pre-war added to the urge for constructive state planning kindled after 1914. But the party was now a divided rump, and his own connection with it hard to take seriously. The more Lloyd George tried to impose his exciting new ideas on the Liberals in the 1920s and 1930s, the

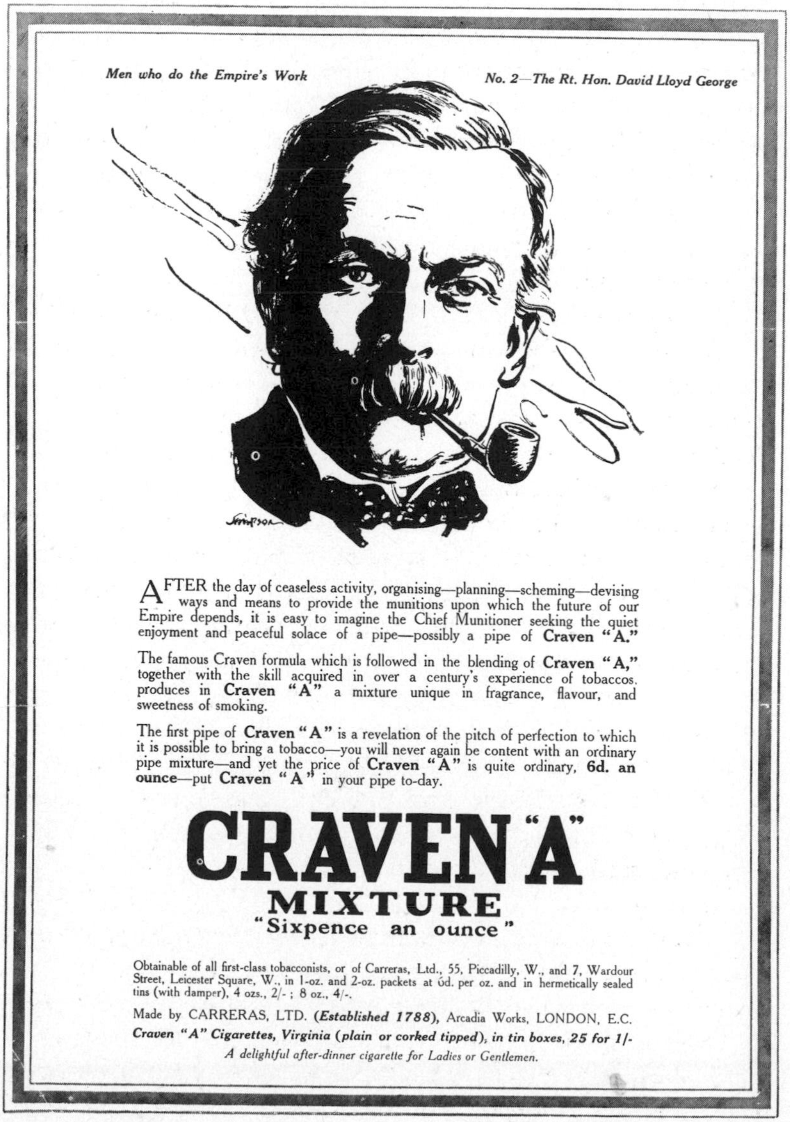

Lloyd George as Munitions Minister 1915–16 lending himself to advertising purposes, a practice then legally permissible and acceptable to public opinion.

more he helped ensure in practice that the Labour Party would supplant them as the voice of the British Left.

The political genius of Lloyd George was not adaptable, without some strain, to the politics of normal times. He was a man for emergencies. As he himself ruefully noted, he was a pilot for the storms and squalls, not for the smooth waters. Perhaps he alone could have surmounted the crisis of Liberalism in 1906 to 1914, harnessing the New Liberalism of social reform to the Old Liberalism of political democracy. Only he could provide the instant leadership needed to steady the nation's nerve during the crisis of world war. Perhaps he too, in his unduly discredited peacetime premiership of 1918 to 1922, was solely capable of directing British policy at home and abroad on lines of moderation and rational reform. If the Jacobins were kept at bay in Britain after 1918, perhaps to the nation's cost, the restoration of the die-hard Bourbons – and Britain was full of them – was warded off also. If there was no general strike, neither was there a counter-revolution. Compared with the turmoil and the inroads into civil liberties that shook Germany, Italy, France, Hungary and other nations after the war, Lloyd George's coalition government does not compare too badly. But thereafter he had no clearly defined political role. His premiership had been a triumph of statecraft, but a failure in terms of political realities. It left him no lifeline to recovery. His only possible escape, joining the Labour Party as Megan was to do after his death, was unthinkable after episodes like Black Friday. After 1922, in fact, he was becoming a political outcast, an easy target for critics in all parties and in none. The abuse that has discredited his reputation and his record ever since shows how lonely he had become, how far removed he seemed to be from the mainstream of British public life.

Yet it may be that the later twentieth century will make him appear, after all, a more contemporary figure than do most of his critics. So many of those critics were securely confident in their faith in Britishness, in British institutions and the British (or rather, English) class system – in the Crown and the empire, in the civil service, in the party system, in a hierarchical educational system, in the careful gradations that mark off rulers from ruled. Perhaps the more permissive, more classless and clear-eyed generation growing up in the 1970s is less shackled by dogma of this kind. To them, perhaps, Lloyd George, with his restless urge for experiment, his distrust for the experts and for established authority, seems in some ways a man ahead of his time. He seems, for instance, relevant today in a way in which

Augustus John's controversial portrait of Lloyd George in 1916.
Bad news from the war front, plus raging toothache may
account for Lloyd George's formidable expression.

Lloyd George as an old man tending his fruit trees at Churt.

Churchill, with his deep fear of the working class and his outmoded attachment to Empire, no longer does, whatever his other great qualities. Lloyd George, unlike Churchill, does not represent a dead past and a decaying society. For the changes he began in our social structure and governmental machinery did not peter out in 1922, even in so conservative a country as Britain. They were not wholly extinguished by the backstairs revolt of the backwoodsmen at the Carlton Club, nor by the sterility of the Baldwin years that followed. They are still in being, ready to be advanced much further. In this sense, the understanding of Lloyd George is not just an academic issue for historians, confined to the hothouse atmosphere of the seminar – though there is still much enlightenment to be offered there. It is, or should be, a theme to fire the faith of those who seek to create in Britain a more truly democratic and just society. For, more than any other prime minister that we have known, Lloyd George, reared in a shoemaker's home in a remote Welsh village, always rooted in the class from which he sprang, belongs to the whole people.

SELECT BIBLIOGRAPHY

ORIGINAL MATERIAL

du Parcq, Herbert, *The Life of David Lloyd George*, vol. IV (1913)
George, William, *My Brother and I* (1958)
Lloyd George, David, *War Memoirs*, 6 vols. (1933–6); *The Truth about the Peace Treaties*, 2 vols. (1938)
Middlemas, Keith (ed.), *Thomas Jones: Whitehall Diary* vols. I–III (1969–71)
Morgan, Kenneth O. (ed.), *Lloyd George: Family Letters, 1885–1936* (1973)
Stevenson, Frances, *The Years that are Past* (1967)
Taylor, A.J.P. (ed.), *Lloyd George: a Diary by Frances Stevenson* (1971)

BIOGRAPHIES

Davies, Watkin, *Lloyd George, 1863–1914* (1939)
Grigg, John, *The Young Lloyd George* (1973)
Jones, Thomas, *Lloyd George* (1951)
Morgan, Kenneth O., *David Lloyd George: Welsh Radical as World Statesman* (1963)
Owen, Frank, *Tempestuous Journey* (1954)
Taylor, A.J.P., *Lloyd George: Rise and Fall* (1961)

BACKGROUND BOOKS

Beaverbrook, Lord, *Politicians and the War, 1914–1916*, 2 vols. (1928), *Men and Power, 1917–1918* (1956), *The Decline and Fall of Lloyd George* (1963)
Blake, Robert, *The Unknown Prime Minister* (1955)
Boyce, George, *Englishmen and Irish Troubles* (1972)
Briggs, Asa, *Seebohm Rowntree* (1961)
Churchill, Randolph, *Winston S. Churchill*, Vol. II (1967)
Clarke, P.F., *Lancashire and the New Liberalism* (1971)
Cowling, Maurice, *The Impact of Labour, 1920–1924* (1971)

Ensor, R. C. K., *England, 1870–1914* (1936)
Gilbert, Martin, *Winston S. Churchill*, vol. III (1971)
Gollin, A. M., *Proconsul in Politics* (1964)
Hazlehurst, Cameron, *Politicians at War, July 1914 to May 1915* (1971)
Jenkins, Roy, *Asquith* (1964)
Jones, Thomas, *A Diary with Letters 1931–50* (1954)
Morgan, Kenneth O., *Wales in British Politics, 1868–1922* (1963); *The Age of Lloyd George* (1971)
Mowat, C. L., *Britain between the Wars 1918–1940* (1955)
Roskill, S. W., *Hankey: Man of Secrets*, vols. I and II (1970–72)
Skidelsky, Robert, *Politicians and the Slump* (1968)
Taylor, A. J. P., *English History, 1914–1945* (1965); *Beaverbrook* (1972); (ed.), *Lloyd George: Twelve Essays* (1971)
Ullman, R. H., *The Anglo-Soviet Accord* (1973)
Wilson, Trevor, *The Downfall of the Liberal Party, 1914–35* (1966); (ed.) *The Political Diaries of C.P. Scott, 1911–28* (1970)

ACKNOWLEDGMENTS

The author would like to acknowledge the helpful comments of the editor, the admirable typing of Miss Pat Lloyd, the invaluable editorial assistance of Miss Ann Wilson of Weidenfeld and Nicolson, and the patience and careful reading of the manuscript by his wife, Jane.

Photographs and illustrations were supplied by and are reproduced by kind permission of the following:
Aberdeen Art Gallery: 214; Associated Press: 186; Bassano & Vandyk Studios: 117, 123*r*, 156; Beaverbrook Library: 16, 19, 24, 76, 86, 99, 106, 112, 116, 118, 133, 136, 137, 151, 169, 175, 195, 204, 216; British Museum: 62, 69, 70, 71, 79, 138, 148, 153, 154, 160; Caernarvonshire Record Office: 25, 28, 30, 33, 34, 42*a* & *b*, 43, 56, 64, 75, 192, 196, 202; Camera Press (photos by Bassano): 2, 102; Fawcett Society, London: 48, 49; William Gordon Davis: 58; Imperial War Museum: 110–11; Manchester Public Libraries: 21; Mansell Collection: 11, 23, 39, 53, 87, 95, 114, 129, 142*b*, 144, 213; National Library of Wales: 9, 12, 27, 31, 73, 91, 199, 207, 210; National Museum of Wales: 105; National Portrait Gallery: 41, 50, 85, 104, 109, 123*l*; Newspaper Collectors' Club: 80; Popperfoto: 67, 88, 159, 171, 172, 187; Radio Times Hulton Picture Library: 13, 14, 17, 45*a* & *b*, 46, 55, 61, 83, 92, 97, 100, 121, 125, 126, 131, 139, 142*a*, 143, 147, 163, 166, 176*a* & *b*, 177*a* & *b*, 180, 182, 185, 189, 193.

Picture research by Carol Glass-Storyk.

INDEX